GW01086142

VERONA

© Copyright by Casa Editrice Bonechi via dei Cairoli 18 b - 50131 Firenze - Italia
Tel. +39 055 576841 - Fax +39 055 5000766
E-mail: bonechi@bonechi.it Internet: www.bonechi.it www.bonechi.com

Publication created and designed by Casa Editrice Bonechi
Editorial management: Serena de Leonardis
Graphic design, picture research and layout: Serena de Leonardis
Make up: Federica Balloni
Cover: Laura Settesoldi
Editing: Patrizia Fabbri
Text: Patrizia Fabbri
Translation: Rodney Lockay, for Globe, Foligno

Collective work. All rights reserved.
No part of this publication may be reproduced or transmitted in any form or by any means,
whether electronic, chemical, mechanical, photocopy, or otherwise
(including cinema, television, and any information storage and retrieval system)
without the express written permission of the publisher.

The cover and layout of this publication are the work of Casa Editrice Bonechi graphic artists and as such are protected by international copyright
and in Italy under Art. 102 of Law No.633 concerning authors' rights.

Printed in Italy by Centro Stampa Editoriale Bonechi.

The majority of the photographs are property of the Casa Editrice Bonechi Archives.

Other photographs were provided by
G. Barone: pages 14a, 24a, 77c, 86a, 89b;
G. Dagli Orti: pages 4, 38b, 39, 40b, 43, 46, 62-67, 78ac, 79abc, 80, 87;
L. Di Giovine: pages 3b, 5b, 6a, 8c, 9bcd, 11b, 12/13, 15b, 16, 21c, 29, 33b, 34, 36ab, 37, 42cd, 47, 48, 50, 51, 53, 56, 57, 58c, 59bc,
75b, 78b, 79d, 82d, 85a, 86bc, 88a, 89a, 90a, 91b, 92b, 93;
M. Fraschetti: page 49;
Randazzo srl - Di Giovine: pages 68/69;
S. Rebuffi: pages 8a, 11a, 35a.

ISBN 88-476-1060-5

* * *

INTRODUCTION

Verona is a truly beautiful city which blends its glorious, centuries-old history with a superbly harmonious urban character. This part of the Po Valley has uninterruptedly been a vital area for communication ever since the remotest of times with the first human settlements. The Brennero road and the course of the Adige river are two such arteries of communication. The first pre-historical settlements rose on the "Collina di San Pietro" next to a narrow point in the river suitable for crossing. This is also where the very first Rhaeto-Etruscan village was to flourish. Polybius, however, records the first contacts between Rome and an inhabited area here only in the fourth century BC. In 148 BC the via Postumia was opened. Not only did this road help to develop further the beginnings of this city, but so too did it put Verona on a direct line between Aquileia and Genoa. Not by chance, therefore, was the first major development of the city's original settlement on the right bank of the Adige River recorded in the second century BC. By the middle of the following century the city received Roman citizenship and sought to give a major impulse to urban development throughout the entire inhabited area. Verona had by then become a strategic outpost and important commercial centre within a system of roads undergoing major development. A truly classical Roman city was thus born which, be-

cause of its specific characteristics, simply grew up on the right bank of the river. This was the lower side of the river and on a plain. The left side was destined to carry out purely celebratory functions. It was, in fact, the perfect site for Verona's theatre and large temple. Within the urban centre the cardo (which now corresponds to via Leoni, via Cappello and via Sant'Egidio) and the decumanus (Corso Porta Borsari and Corso Sant'Anastasia) met up in the Forum which was, more or less, where Piazza delle Erbe is today. The housing blocks seemed to be arranged in a regular grid of straight streets which were either parallel or perpendicular to each other. This grid can still be discerned in the ancient city centre. Where the river itself did not protect the city, walls were raised around the inhabited area with two large gates. By the first century AD, however, these same walls could no longer contain the city's rapidly growing population and urban development. Such development continued outside the Roman walls with the building of the impressive "Arco dei Gavi" and, above all, the amphitheatre. Much later when the threat of barbarian invasion became apparent, in 265 AD emperor Gallienus decided to protect the entire city with huge fortifications.

After the fall of the Roman Empire, Verona became the capital of the Ostrogoth and Longobard dominions. Such renewed responsibility did not, however, seem to have particular repercussions on the urban structure. What did modify the urban structure in a decisive fashion was the appearance of monastic settlements in the city such as San Giovanni in Valle, Santa Maria in Organo and San Fermo Maggiore. Together with the monumental nucleus of the cathedral and San Zeno, these monastic settlements ended up becoming the main points of reference within the urban fabric of the mediaeval city. In the course of the centuries, Verona often suffered huge losses, for example, at the hands of the Hungarians in the tenth century and because of the plagues which would repeatedly jeopardise its very existence. Despite these setbacks, however, Verona continued

to flourish because of its rapidly expanding economy, its enviable geographic position and the entrepreneurial character of its busy merchant trade. Even when the Adige river dramatically overflowed its banks in the ninth century and shifted its own bed causing disastrous effects on the city, growth continued and the river itself remained an important resource. Verona as a free commune embarked on the construction of bridges and new, wider defence mechanisms such as the opening of numerous canals next to the course of the famous Adigetto to protect the outermost parts of the city.

Ezzelino da Romano was the political leader of the communal city of Verona between 1232 and 1259. Even though members of the Della Scala family had formerly occupied public offices, in 1259 when Mastino I of the powerful Della Scala family from Verona took over, communal freedom fell. Mastino I Della Scala succeeded Ezzelino first of all as "podestà" or leader of the Commune, then as captain of the people. When he finally became the effective lord of the city he inaugurated a period of splendour for a dynasty which was to last right through to the fifteenth century. Henry VII officially recognised it as the ruling family not only of Verona but also of the other territories it was to conquer. Dante was to remain eternally grateful to this family for having been able to spend part of his exile there under the protection of Bartolomeo I and his brother Cangrande I. The Della Scala family significantly reorganised the urban structure of Verona building elegant monuments which might celebrate their power. Alberto I and Cangrande I endowed the city with another wall which surrounded an area of fallow land so as to allow for further urban development. In the middle of the fourteenth century Cangrande II patronised the building of Castelvecchio which, together with its bridge, represented above all a defence against possible internal enemies. The plans of the Della Scala family also included the very heart of the city such as Piazza delle Erbe and Piazza dei Signori. At the same time, the wool trade and commerce underwent systematic, progressive development. In 1387 Gian Galeazzo Visconti conquered the city, but the Della Scala family soon found their way back to power. Shortly afterwards, however, the Della Scala family lost this power forever when the Venetian Republic took over in 1405.

The dominion of the Serenissima, though decisive from the political point of view, did not significantly modify, however, the architectural identity of Verona as the Della Scala family had left it. In the sixteenth century, however, a strong artistic personality came to the fore, Michele Sanmicheli. This was when the first major urban modifications were carried out, such as the dismantlement of the military citadel which had been built by the Visconti family in the southern part of the city. This part went back to cultivating its ancient residential character with the building of fine town houses for the gentry under the architectural guidance of Sanmicheli himself. The walls around this area were strengthened and widened. The overall result was a complete metamorphosis of large tracts of urban living. Because of the terrible plague of 1630 and the Serenissima's systematic attempt to limit and circumscribe the terra ferma nobility, Verona underwent stagnation and contraction during the seventeenth century. In a reaction to this imposed isolation, the leading classes of Verona sought to increase their merchant trade. As a result, Verona turned more and more from military action to commercial endeavour making the most of its extremely fertile farmlands.

Such waning insistence upon the strategic importance of the city allowed for the dismantlement of the defence systems. At the same time urban living became more and more comfortable and spacious, especially with the definition of the whole area of the Bra. Administration too underwent radical transformation. At the turn of the nineteenth century certain foreign dominions were established in the city. In 1796 the French occupied Verona. In 1801 the treaty of Lunéville divided the city between the Austrians and those north of the Alps but in 1805 the French returned to be its undisputed official rulers. In 1814, however, on a European level it was decided that Verona should be given back to the Habsburgs. Once more under Austrian rule, Verona was then to carry out yet again its ancient military function by using its strategic importance to defend the Austrian possessions in Italy. The undeferrable requirements of war deemed necessary that military rigour should soon profoundly characterise the life of this extraordinarily dynamic city in both its urban fabric and economy. Only with the annexation to the Kingdom of

Italy in 1866 would Verona regain an urban dimension more respectful of its history and happier economic prospects. A widespread programme of industrial development was carried out in parallel with a radical rethinking of urban building. After the disastrous floods of 1882 which caused the erection of the unique containing walls and the disappearance of the picturesque world moving about on the banks of the river, work was also carried out to more rationally direct the flow of the Adige river. During the twentieth century the city's population grew so much that it could no longer be contained by the walls built so many centuries beforehand. This demographic overflow colonised the outer-lying areas, very often, however, in a chaotic fashion. The city was heavily damaged during the Second World War, especially due to bombing. Immediately afterwards, however, in 1945, an articulated plan was made ready to re-build what had been torn to pieces. During the following decades a policy was implemented so as to revitalise the historical centre together with its artistic and architectural patrimony. Even though such guided intervention often gives rise to heated debate and varying interpretations of what ought to be done, this policy is still being carried out today.

Today Verona is an important commercial crossroads. It is the second most-important business centre in the Veneto Region with its activities ranging throughout a whole series of fields, especially agriculture and industry. The industrial sectors, in fact, are extremely diversified, going from the preparation of agricultural products and marble, to shoes and leather goods, clothing and the confectionery industry. The services sector is also especially strong. The city is, furthermore, the seat of prestigious fairs and expos, such as the "Fiera dell'Agricoltura", which is the most important in Europe, and the renowned "Vinitaly".

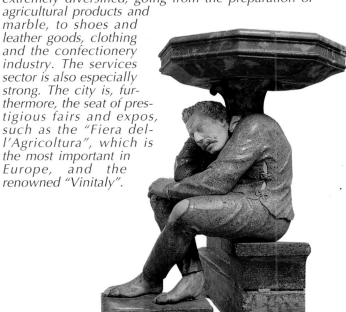

PIAZZA BRA

The third and last centre of the economic and social life of the city is **Piazza Bra**. The name derives from the term *braida* in Veronese meaning "open space". This is the largest square in all of Verona opening out in front of the majestic Arena in the area once set aside for the *Forum Boarium* or cattle market in Roman times. It has a monumental setting with a sixteenth-century layout deriving from the work of Sanmicheli. This includes the famous *Portoni della Bra* or Gates of the Bra which are two mighty-looking arches with battlements built in the sixteenth century on top of the buildings which once made up the fourteenth-century wall of the city commissioned by Gian Galeazzo Visconti. The lush green garden in the middle of the square contains the *fountain of the Alps*, the *monument to Victor Emanuel II* (1883) and the one built in the twentieth-century to commemorate the partisans. The perimeter of the square is rather irregular. Despite this, the fine buildings surrounding Piazza Bra enclose it much like a crown. These noteworthy buildings, specifically built either for private noble families or for public use, were part of Sanmicheli's original plan, such as **Palazzo della Gran Guardia** and **Palazzo Barbieri**. **Palazzo Guastaverza**, for example, was designed directly by Sanmicheli himself. The buildings are lined up in a curve which leads to the famous ***Listone*** which is a long footpath where the people of Verona delight in taking their strolls.

The spacious and always crowded Listone. To the right, the outermost wing of the Arena can just be seen.
Left, the famous towering capital of Piazza Bra.

Piazza Bra and the Listone are characterised by the elegance of the long series of fine buildings around them. The buildings have elegant façades rich in original decorations and terraces looking out directly on to the street.

The Palazzo della Gran Guardia

This building was begun in 1610 on the southern side of the square but was finally completed only as late as 1820. **Palazzo della Gran Guardia** is the work of Domenico Curtoni even though quite a few architectural characteristics definitely point in the direction of certain tastes deriving from Sanmicheli. Its majestic appearance today is particularly ennobled by an elegant *portico* placed within an austere setting of ashlarwork. A long series of windows counterbalances the otherwise heavy look of the imposing structure.

Palazzo Barbieri

This building is also known as the *Palazzo della Gran Guardia Nuova*. Today it houses the Municipio (municipal offices). It is a fine nineteenth-century construction with an obvious air of neo-classicism, that is, with explicit references to the monumental grandeur of ancient Roman temples. It was built in 1838 under the supervision of G. Barbieri.

The characteristic Gates of the Bra crowned with merlons; the Fountain of the Alps beneath the monument to Victor Emanuel II, in Piazza Bra gardens; the Palazzo della Gran Guardia with its long elegant series of windows.

The characteristic neo-classical architecture of Palazzo Barbieri, now the seat of the Municipal Offices.

The Philharmonic Theatre

Near the Portoni della Bra there lies one of the most prestigious institutions of the entire city, not to mention the most important theatre in the city – the **Philharmonic Theatre**. It was initially designed and built in 1716 by Francesco Bibiena, a famous architect and scenographer of the time. Fifty-four years later, however, it was completely burnt down in a fire but entirely re-built afterwards. The theatre which can be admired today is not, however, the second theatre but the third inasmuch as in 1945 bombing razed it to the ground leaving only the atrium and foyer intact. These were then restored and integrated, together with the original eighteenth-century plan, into the new building we can see today. This is thanks to the Accademia Filarmonica and the careful planning of the architect V. Filippini. This is one of the most loved theatres in all of Verona. Indeed, it is one of the most vital cultural institutions of the city itself.

The Maffei Epigraphic Museum

Another famous institution of the city of Verona edging onto Piazza Bra is without doubt the **Maffei Epigraphic Museum**. It was built in 1714 by Scipione Maffei according to the designing and planning of the architect A. Pompei. It can be entered though the monumental pronaos comprising of six columns. It houses an extraordinary collection of inscriptions in stone and other materials, not to mention urns, statues and vases not only of Roman and Greek origin, but also of Italic provenance together with findings from all over the Veneto Region. This is without doubt a collection of immense historical and archaeological value. The collection was built up very slowly at first, but with great passion, by Nichesola. It became a truly major collection when he started adding mediaeval artefacts to it.

Below, the majestic six column pronaos solemnly acts as an entrance to the Maffei Museum of Lapidary Inscriptions, which is a veritable Veronese institution. Relief work with elegant mythological friezes and sculptures, together with stone tablets and urns of Italic, Greek and Roman origin found in several different archaeological sites of the Veneto region, comprise the priceless historical-artistic treasures of the Maffei Epigraphic Museum.

L'ARENA (The Amphitheatre)

Between the ancient and mediaeval walls there is an open area popularly known as the *Bra*. The term derives from ancient Germanic *breit* meaning broad. It is here that the **Amphitheatre** stands. This is without doubt the biggest and best preserved Roman monument in an absolute sense. It is more commonly known as the Arena. This was where gladiators would fight and where all circus and equestrian events were held. It is currently situated two metres below street level with only two orders of arches. Actually, today we can see only a part of the original amphitheatre, the *ala*. The original edifice was built up into three orders of marble arches over thirty metres high. On top on this there was also a crowning wall with square windows which can still be seen in some etchings by Palladio. This Renaissance architect painstakingly studied the monument and made similar buildings based on what was left in his day here, at the Colosseum in Rome and the Amphitheatre in Pola.

The Arena was, therefore, originally built in the first century AD outside the Republican walls of the city. It was articulated into four concentric, elliptic rings whose internal axes were respectively 73 and 44 metres and whose external axes, including the outermost wall which has almost disappeared altogether, measure 152 and 123 metres in length. The 44 marble tiers gave rise to a 40 metre mass supported by arches and walls placed on the four rings the outermost of which, as has been said above, simply carried out the function of façade. The wing remaining to testify to the overall grandeur in ancient times still boasts its four arches per level, but originally it must

The Arena of Verona is also unusual because of the excellent state of conservation of its cavea. This is due to the solid nature of the supporting structures in stone together with the care originally taken in choosing the materials.

At the feet of the double series of arches making up the curved walls of the Arena of Verona some traces of the ancient walls built by Gallienus can still be seen.

have had 73 pillars built out of so-called Veronese stone. This special stone came from the area around Sant'Ambrogio in Valpolicella and was systematically used for gates and other monuments datable in the first century AD. Every pillar was square with 2 metre wide sides. Together they formed 72 arched openings on every level which each had a 4.4 m wide corridor running around the second ring which is now openly visible. Though dressed in stone, the ring was built up of a hardy conglomerate called *opus coementicum* composed of cement, river pebbles and brick or roof tile fragments. These building materials would be poured into giant moulds so as to build up the vaults, arches and walls. Huge blocks of stone would then be placed against the structure as in the "titanic walls". Another corridor 3 m wide gives rise to the fourth, innermost ring entirely built of brick 3.6 m thick. By looking through any one of the 72 arched openings it is possible to behold the perspective fugue lines running through ever-smaller pillar and vaults right to the farthest openings composed of two vertical monoliths and a horizontal one acting as architrave. These then lead the eye to the innermost ring which opens up into the gallery or pit and cavea. Here there are ramps of internal stairs leading to the wide tiers in the middle of the openings called *vomitoria*. On the whole, the Arena is an exceptionally solid structure. Built entirely of stone and brick, it has been capable for almost twenty centuries of supporting the enormous marble basin. This typically Roman structure is, therefore, like the Colosseum and the Provençal amphitheatres of Nîmes and Arles, not to mention those of Frejus, Pola and Aosta.

The Arena of Verona is third in size of its type, coming after the Colosseum and the Amphitheatre of Santa Maria Capua Vetere. It is, however, certainly the most interesting due to the outstanding state of conservation of the cavea. This honour derives from the careful choice of building materials and the solid nature of the load-bearing structures. Indeed other amphitheatres, such as those in Padua and Rimini, were built in brick. Furthermore, though constantly being used, throughout the centuries the Arena has also been the object of constant care. One of its first and most illustrious restorers was king Theodoric. In 1222, Rizzardo, count of San Bonifacio and podestà or political leader of the Free Municipality of Verona, donated his own money for repairs. In 1228 certain communal statutes introduced a tax of 200 lira per year towards the maintenance of the Arena. It was under the Republic of Venice that the four arches which had collapsed in the sixteenth century were then rebuilt. The Arena, much like the Colosseum, was also, however, considered a handy quarry for ready-made blocks of stone for other walls and palaces. Fortunately this did not create much damage overall because generally only the stones fallen from the top wing were re-used elsewhere. These pieces had fallen because of the passage of time and/or earthquake. They still bear witness to their origins, however, thanks to the inscriptions then made on them.

There are also other reasons for the good state of the Arena. One such reason is the perfect system of hydraulic drainage. Within this "mountain of stone" the system perfectly gathers and leads away any water fil-

The ancient Arena of Verona is smaller in size only to the Colosseum and Santa Maria Capua Vetere.
It may no longer be as big as it was in ancient times, but it certainly still maintains its original elegance and magnificence.
Only a small segment of the outermost architectural ring remains. It has four arches on every level and
still stands out to dominate the entire monument.

An evocative particular of the only portion left of the outermost architectural ring originally comprising the amphitheatre. The solid nature of the structure is not, however, without a certain austere elegance.

tering down into it through internal veins or the *vomitoria*. Each of the three ring corridors and the base of the external platform have an underground drainage system running. The gallery is crossed by two other drains which lead to the outside. Underneath the intersection of these two drains there is an area set aside 34 m long, 8.85 m wide and 2 m deep, originally covered in stone slabs. This veritable navel of Verona, built by an unknown architect in the first decades of the first century AD and embellished with archways, tunnels, obscure holes running through it, cyclopic walls and unexpected openings, stimulated the fantasy and imagination of the people of Verona during the Middle Ages. Diabolical stories were thus invented of Faustian pacts between ambitious knights and Mephistopheles in order to explain the existence of what was to become known as the "labyrinth" much like the Theatre.

Going back to ancient times, however, some literary and archaeological evidence is extant pertaining to the gladiator fights being regularly shown at the Arena. Indeed, in Verona there was even a school for gladiator fighting. On the other hand, instead, there is no concrete evidence to suggest that the martyrdom of Christians had ever taken place, even though this is very likely. In the following twenty centuries there were to be, however, many heretics burnt at the stake, "judgements of God", ordeals, tournaments, whirls, jousts and, especially popular right up to the nineteenth century, bull-fights.

During the nineteenth century the Arena also held circus events and witnessed the preparation of hot-air balloons and the production of theatrical pieces held on a small stage. On this very stage comic actors from Carlo Goldoni's company would often perform. Even a very young Eleonora Duse climbed onto this humble stage to play the part of Juliet. Gabriele D'Annunzio was to record this fact in his own works. Still during the nineteenth century, opera came to the Arena as matinee performances.

Below, a view of Piazza Bra in an aquatint by C. Ferrari.

A photo taken in 1916 documenting the first market held in the Arena on 17 April. It was meant to protect the public from First World War air raids.

Amongst the many shown there was the *Barbiere di Siviglia* by Rossini and *L'elisir d'amore* by Donizetti. Only in 1913 was the Arena to be consecrated as the greatest lyric theatre of the world with a huge stage and seating for some 20,000 spectators per evening. That year was the hundredth anniversary of the birth of Giuseppe Verdi and Verona was about to celebrate it. It was decided that *Aida* should be played. Shortly afterwards the stage, stalls and show were built in with the army supplying the electric lighting. The three-dimensional scenes, which were designed and made by a young architect, Ettore Faginoli, proved to be an authentic revelation. The entire show overall was a triumph and drew in crowds of spectators from all over Europe.

Since then opera has been regularly shown at the Arena of Verona. It has become an international event inasmuch as the opera season manages to draw over half a million people every year. The ancient Amphitheatre of Roman origin is now living through a second youth. Its functionality and fascination have well stood the test of time in two thousand years of its eventful yet ever-noble existence.

PIAZZA DELLE ERBE

The picturesque **Piazza delle Erbe** has always been the historical and monumental centre of Verona. Indeed, it corresponds to the urban area set aside in ancient times for the Roman Forum. It is still one of the most celebrated and animated areas of all of Verona. This is also where, for example, the terribly busy *fruit and vegetable market* takes place. Its unmistakable hallmark is the veritable sea of huge umbrellas protecting the market. In the shade of these umbrellas, it is possible to acquaint oneself with the most authentic, outgoing nature of the people of Verona. The square is loved by artists and poets alike and is ennobled by a crown of beautiful buildings. When these buildings were constructed at the height of the communal age around the twelfth and thirteenth centuries, the original Roman forum was drastically reduced in size to what it is today. The most famous of these buildings are the *Palazzo Comunale* (Municipal Chambers), the *Domus Mercatorum*, the *Torre dei Lamberti*. The *Fountain of Our Lady Verona*, the *Domus Nova* (original premises of the *Podestà* or elected mayor in mediaeval times, but heavily restored in the seventeenth and eighteenth centuries), *Casa Mazzanti* with its interesting sixteenth century allegorical fres-

Piazza delle Erbe is constantly brought back to life with the hustle and bustle of the fruit and vegetable market. The square constitutes the true historical centre of Verona. It is closed off at one end by the profile of the Lion of St. Mark and the elegant architecture of Palazzo Maffei. The Gardello Tower rises above.

coes on the façade by Alberto Cavalli, *Casa Cristani*, the *Domus Bladorum* and *Palazzo Mazzanti*. There is also the sixteenth century *marble column* made by Michele Leoni which proudly bears the *Lion of St. Mark*. The Lion was knocked down in revolutionary times, but a copy was subsequently made and re-mounted during the nineteenth century. The elegant square shaped shrine is commonly known as the *Berlina*.

Il Palazzo Comunale

The various wings of **Palazzo Comunale** (Municipal Chambers) look out onto three different city squares, namely Piazza delle Erbe, Piazza dei Signori and Cortile del Mercato Vecchio. Over the centuries, the Palazzo Comunale has undergone profound transformation in its appearance. Its façade in Piazza delle Erbe became decidedly neo-classical in the nineteenth century thanks to the architect Barbieri, whereas its façade in Piazza dei Signori had taken on Renaissance characteristics in the sixteenth century. The Palazzo is a large, square building whose original mediaeval architecture has been preserved only within its inner courtyard. Here there are the characteristic rounded arches supported by solid square pillars, not to mention the typical Veronese use of tufa and brickwork placed in white and red stripes on the outside walls. The *façades* have a narrow appearance thanks to the presence of mullioned windows with several lights and small arches above supported by columns in local red marble. The arches and pillars, which lead to the porticos, are developed on three sides. They also carry out the function of making the entire building seem lighter. Further grace and elegance is conferred via a series of small arches in brickwork supported by a stone corbel and situated under the eaves. In the pillars made with roughly hewn ashlars another typically Veronese characteristic can be seen, destined to be repeated even in subsequent architectural styles: this is without doubt the decisive influence of the Roman amphitheatre, the massive Arena. The **Torre dei Lamberti** is the bell tower of the Palazzo Comunale. Its height is proportional to the size of the Palazzo itself. Building began in 1172 under the guidance of the Lamberti family, hence its own name. The first part of the tower is Romanesque, built as it is with the characteristic bands of brick and tufa. It was to reach its final height of 83 m with a concomitant and surprisingly harmonious succession of styles and building materials. The last section to be added, of course, was the bell loft. This occurred in 1464. Ever since the earliest moments of its existence, the tower was referred to with the name "delle campane" (of the bells) in honour of the bells installed there in 1294 and still there today.

The sixteenth century frescoes of the façade of Mazzanti House.

A wing of the austere Municipal Building stands over Piazza delle Erbe, at the feet of the lofty Lamberti Tower.

La Domus Mercatorum

The **Domus Mercatorum** or Merchant House is a fine Romanesque building which a questionable attempt at restoration in the nineteenth century crowned with improbable Gothic battlements. The Guilds and Corporations of Verona had their first premises placed here right in front of the Palazzo Comunale. In other words, economic power faced political power. The *Domus* we see today was built by Alberto I in 1301 under the Della Scala family. The structure is in stone and brick and in the form of a loggia supported by arches and ennoble by mullioned windows with two lights. Prior to this building, however, there had been another one built in 1210 under Realdo dalle Carceri who was the Podestà (elected mayor in mediaeval times). This earlier one had been built in wood as was the wide-spread custom in Verona and elsewhere at the time. The custom was based on resources - huge quantities of building timber were available in what was thought to be the seemingly endless woods running right through the surrounding countryside.

The Domus Mercatorum is surmounted by arches and delightful mullioned windows. The crown of merlons was added in the nineteenth century. Made in brick and stone, the building housed the town guilds and corporations.

The slim, picturesque Market Column.

The Fountain of Our Lady Verona

At the centre of Piazza delle Erbe the most singular Gothic monument ever created under the Della Scala family can be admired - the **Fountain of Our Lady Verona**. Erected in 1368 by the untiring Cansignorio, the fountain became almost immediately the leading symbol of the city. Cansignorio was stimulated by a precocious humanistic drive concerning art but also by a more pragmatic intention to celebrate the restoration and reactivation of the city's aqueduct. He commissioned the work from the genius of urban architecture, Giovanni Rigino, who used one of the last remaining Roman statues still standing in the Capitolium of Verona. It was a statue of a young woman. For the occasion, he had to remodel her head and arms which by then had fallen into a bad state of disrepair. He then placed her on a marble base very similar to an elegant cup decorated with eight heads arranged in two tiers. Water is channelled from the springs of Avesa across Ponte Pietra. It falls into a wide dish made of porphyry and similar to the one seen in San Zeno. Not by chance do they both come from the ancient Roman thermal baths. The water finally falls onto a base of pink marble closed off by a gathering channel. The scroll which Madonna Verona holds in her hands reads as follows: *Est justi latrix urbs haec et laudi amatrix*. This municipal motto can be translated perhaps as such: This city is the bearer of justice and the lover of praise.

The Fountain of Our Lady Verona, in the exact centre of Piazza delle Erbe. With its ancient Roman statue, the fountain is one of the monuments most cherished by the people of Verona.

The Berlina

The shrine erected in the middle of Piazza delle Erbe, and more commonly known as the **Berlina**, was where the ceremonial investiture of every new *podestà* officially took place. Later on, also other analogous and even more important magistratures were inaugurated here. Taking possession of the office represented a solemn moment and came to be indicated with the term *insediamento* or installation because the new magistrate was taking possession of a *sedia* which was a chair in stone placed within the marble shrine in the shade supported by four marble pillars and elevated by three steps. The *Berlina* we can see today, however, is not the original one. Despite this, it can be noted, though, that on the steps and on one of the sixteenth century pillars the units of measurement in force in Verona since the days of communal government until the introduction of the decimal system are still legible. The "mattone" (brick) and the "tegola" (rule) are outlined on one of the steps in the shape of a rectangle, "el quarel" and of a trapezium, "el copo", the "coppo" on which one could check the size of bricks placed on sale in the square. Any irregularity in the size would be punished via the imposition of heavy fines. From one of the pillars hangs the chain which held the iron ring which could be opened to contain the exact standard of the "fassina" or "fascina", the faggot or bundle of firewood placed on sale. Grooves on the same pillar could also be seen. These were the standard units of length, the "pertica", (rod) the "passo" (step) and the "ponte" (bridge).

Palazzo Maffei

Palazzo Maffei is a imposing building. Its characteristic forms are Baroque and go back to the seventeenth century. They cover, however, a pre-existing thirteenth century structure. Like a veritable monumental curtain, Palazzo Maffei closes off one side of Piazza delle Erbe. It culminates in an agile balcony decorated with *statues* of six divinities (Jupiter, Apollo, Venus, Minerva, Mercury and Hercules). The eminently theatrical function of the façade is also reflected on the inside in the elegant *courtyard* and magnificent *spiralling staircase*. The building originally belonged to the Dal Verme family but was later bought by Erasmo da Narni. This valorous condottiere went down into history with the name Gattamelata. The building itself is overshadowed by the austere yet imposing size of the **Torre del Gardello**. This tower was built entirely in brick in 1370 by Cansignorio della Scala. The apex, however, was added only in 1626.

From the top, the characteristic shrine known as the Berlina; a particular of the shrine of the Market Column; Palazzo Maffei culminating in a balcony decorated with six statues of divinities. It is just as magnificent on the inside.

PIAZZA DEI SIGNORI

This is the other end of the social spectrum of the urban fabric of the ancient city of Verona. Almost complementary to Piazza delle Erbe, **Piazza dei Signori** is different in shape and style. Its aristocratic features and elegant harmony endow it with the unmistakable characteristics of the privileged meeting place for the well to do of the city. There are many fine buildings surrounding this square, such as the Renaissance wing of *Palazzo Comunale*, the eighteenth side of *Domus Nova*, the **Loggia del Consiglio** and the **Palazzo del Capitano**. The **Palazzo degli Scaligeri** is unmistakable with its Ghibelline battlements. From here access can be gained to the elegant internal courtyard of the Palazzo Comunale otherwise known as **Cortile del Mercato Vecchio**. The monumental nature of the courtyard is increased by the double flight of stairs in an agile Gothic style. These flights of stairs are more commonly known as the *"Stairs of Reason"* and it is here that there stands the monument to Dante Alighieri. The monument was created by Ugo Zannoni in 1865 to celebrate the memory of the great poet who was taken in as a permanent guest by the Della Scala family in Verona between 1303 and 1316, that is, during the years of his exile.

Piazza dei Signori is without doubt one of the most beautiful historical areas of Verona. It is surrounded by a wing of the Municipal Buildings, surmounted by the Lamberti Tower, and the prestigious buildings constituting the mediaeval and Renaissance heart of the city of Verona, such as the Domus Nova which housed the Podestà. In the centre of the square there stands the monument to Dante Alighieri, erected in 1865 by Ugo Zannoni.

The Courtyard of the Old Market, in the shadow of the lofty Lamberti Tower, stands with its extremely elegant fifteenth century Scala della Ragione. Its double ramp of steps is embellished with decorative sculptures. The Romanesque Courtyard is surrounded by round archways made lighter in architectural form by the presence of windows with three lights.

The House of the Della Scala Family

The **Palazzo della Prefettura** (Seat of the Prefecture) corresponds to the old Della Scala Palace which was begun in the twelfth century but was completed only in the fourteenth century. It underwent, therefore, several major changes in design and style but was accurately restored and brought back to its original structure in the first few decades of the twentieth century. In the austere *courtyard* there features a double loggia with ogival and round arches dating back to the original building. There is, furthermore, a magnificent well-curb which is a typical manifestation of the Renaissance culture assimilated by the stone-masons of Verona. On the inside of the House, instead, there is nothing left of the old splendours. Altichiero da Verona and Avanzo in 1364 fresco painted the entire *Sala Grande* (Great Hall) with a celebration of the military feats of the Della Scala family.

The Loggia del Consiglio

The **Palazzo del Consiglio** is an example of refined elegance and architectural wisdom. It was built to face the Piazza between 1475 and 1492. Better known under as *Loggia of Brother Giocondo*, it is normally attributed, though with some founded reservation, to Giocondo, a Domenican monk and excellent architect. At first Giocondo was contended over on the one hand by the papal court of Rome in a time of great architectural renovation and, on the other, by the royal court of France. He was analogously fought over by Venice and Naples where he found several opportunities to display his prowess. At the base of second order pillar of the loggia towards Via Fogge, a man can be seen sculptured with a beard and cap on his head. Popular tradition has it that this sculptured man is Brother Giocondo. Experts are slightly more critical and reluctant to support this interpretation. They do admit, however, though with extreme caution, that such a phenomenon is not impossible. After all, this Dominican monk is considered to be the founding father of Renaissance architecture in the Veneto area. Whoever the real author might have been, the Loggia or Palazzo del Consiglio still remains an admirable feat in architecture with the perfect proportions of its eight *arches* articulated between elegant columns in pink and grey marble resting on a balustrade. The upper level corresponds to the *room* especially designated for the Council meetings. Light enters into it through four mullioned windows with two lights with corresponding semicircular gables above. The space between the windows is articulated in turn by pilaster strips on which traces of gilding can still be seen. The pilaster strips enclose areas frescoed to resemble polychromatic marble whereas the medallions frame imperial heads. The cornice above supports five *statues* by Alberto da Milano. These statues represent the five most illustrious men from Verona in Roman times: Catullus, Pliny, Marcus, Vitruvius, Cornelius Nepos. Under the arcade on the architrave above the door leading to the staircase, it is still possible to read the gold letters carved in the stone. The letters make up the motto which Venice granted Verona: *Pro summa fide summus amor*, "because of great faith, great love".

The elegant Council Loggia with its eight arches resting on a long balustrade and statues of illustrious citizens of Verona crown the eaves. The double windows are separated by fresco work and pilaster strips.

The Palazzo del Capitano

The imposing **Palazzo del Capitano** stands out beneath a fourteenth-century tower with battlements. An elegant *portal* created by Sanmicheli opens up in the sixteenth-century façade. This building derives its name from the historical role carried out by the elected major or "captain" of Verona in these official premises in the time of Venetian dominion. The building probably came to have this particular appearance due to the coming together of various different and pre-existing town tower-houses. The Palazzo del Capitano boasts a magnificent inner courtyard onto which the *Loggia Barbaro* and the *Porta Bombardiera* look out. The *Porta Bombardiera* was built in 1687 and immediately came to be known with this unusual name because of its decoration which is purely based on war being, as it is, entirely made up of reproductions of weapons.

The Church of Santa Maria Antica

Santa Maria Antica is a church of small dimensions surmounted by a tiny bell-tower. It is known above all for having the palace chapel of the Della Scala family. Its origins are, however, much older and perhaps date back to the seventh century, that is, well before the period of greatest splendour for this dynasty. The building can hardly be said to be famous for any works of particular relevance. Despite this, the nave and two aisles inside do seem to be pervaded by an austere atmosphere. Indeed the entire complex perfectly exemplifies the period of Romanesque architecture in Verona, especially in the characteristic bands alternating in stone and brick. The well-known name of this church derives, therefore, almost entirely from the fact that the church houses the authentic private cemetery of the lords of Verona. The cemetery in turn is monumental and quite impressive due to the presence of the tombs of the Della Scala family.

The church of Santa Maria Antica: whereas the outside is characterised by an imposing canopy covering the tomb of Cangrande, that is, the equestrian statue standing on the spire the original of which is in the Museo di Castelvecchio, the inside is simple and austere, imbued with an arcane atmosphere.

Cangrande's fears

Cangrande II Della Scala, son of Mastino II and lord of Verona from 1351 to 1359, decided to have Castelvecchio built more out of protection from internal enemies than from foreign adversaries. Such was the case during his short reign when he was forced to undermine a conspiracy set against him by his half-brother Fregnano, Mastino's illegitimate son. His attempts at self-preservation were ultimately to be thwarted, however, when he was only twenty-seven years old. His other brother, Cansignorio, eight years his younger, had him murdered and then succeeded him on the throne.

LE ARCHE SCALIGERE

Right next to the Church of Santa Maria Antica stand the impressive Della Scala Tombs. These funeral monuments still succeed in creating an authentic and indeed elegant encampment of noble knights. Within a space enclosed by a marble wall stand two pavilions veiled by an iron railing which is, in fact, an extremely refined lace of iron marked over and over again with the emblem of the heraldic scala or ladder. The third one is hanging above the door of the temple. Other tombs still of a more classical sarcophagus style can be seen lying on the ground but always within the enclosed space. One's attention, however, concentrates of the three hanging tombs. Two of these in particular constitute a fine example of the most successful form of Gothic craftsmanship within the school of Verona. Such an example is elegant and ornate, but always

The Della Scala tombs are closed off by an elegant wrought iron fence in which the heraldic motif of the Della Scala family is repeated. The area is set out like a military encampment and constitutes the official cemetery of the members of this family. A holy warrior stands on every corner pilaster protected by a spire-shaped canopy which seems to be watching over the eternal rest of these Lords. The two most important tombs, complete with canopy and a veritable profusion of decorative sculptures, belong to Cansignorio (bottom right) and Mastino II (bottom left).

Equestrian monuments crown the Tomb of Cansignorio (bottom), and the Tomb of Mastino II (below right).

mindful of the classical Romanesque style. They are attributed to the expert work of Giovanni Rigino. Some critics beg to differ and would prefer to ascribe it more cautiously to an otherwise unknown "Maestro delle Arche Scaligere" (Master of the Della Scala Tombs). The tomb of Cangrande I della Scala, who died in 1329, is considered to be one the finest examples of fourteenth sculpture in Verona. It is placed on high above the side door of the church. The sarcophagus is embellished with scenes of war and supports the tall marble reproduction of the body of Cangrande I who is smiling in his eternal sleep whilst lying on his field bed. At the top of the spire, above the Gothic canopy, Cangrande can still be seen smiling protected, as he is, by his weapons and from the safety of his horse elegantly harnessed for a tournament whose saddle-cloth seems to be flapping in the wind. The equestrian statue we admire today is, however, only a copy. The original is preserved in the Museo di Castelvecchio. The other tomb created by the chisel of Giovanni Rigino or by the unknown "Maestro delle Arche Scaligere" belongs to Mastino II who died in 1351. This prince had personally overseen, however, the execution of this work. Angels and saints watch over the rich sarcophagus which still shows traces of painting and gilding. The prince himself is sitting on his horse at the top of the monument in full armour. His face is covered by the closed helmet surmounted by a crest in the shape of a dog's head and suitably decorated with the wings of an eagle to represent his status as imperial vicar. The third tomb is of the Lombard school and constitutes an example of the work carried out and signed by Gaspare Broaspini and Bonino da Campione (1375) who had also created the Milanese sepulchre of Barnabò Visconti. It is hexagonal in shape, unlike the square ones executed previously, and rests on six twisting columns. Its six façades are richly decorated with statues, ornamentation, relief-work, spires and pinnacles typical of the international Gothic style. Cansignorio lies there watched over by holy warriors in full armour. On a pedestal rising above the hexagonal, pyramid-shaped spire, Cansignorio is sitting on his horse without a saddle-cloth. He seems to be waiting to take on his final assault. He is brandishing his lance and is wearing simple armour in chain-mail which covers his head but not his astonished face. His sallet is without ornamentation. The other sepulchres which comprise the monumental cemetery belong to Mastino I, Alboino, Bartolomeo, Alberto I and Cangrande II.

Juliet's house with its characteristic balcony and the romantic bronze statue dedicated to the young girl by N. Costantini and now standing in the inner courtyard of her supposed house.

Juliet's house

William Shakespeare set one of his most celebrated tragedies in the picturesque atmosphere of mediaeval Verona. He thus immortalised the desperate love shared by two young people ineluctably divided by the rivalry between the two respective families. Today it is still possible to find consistent traces of the moving story of Romeo and Juliet. Not far from Piazza delle Erbe, for example, there is Via Cappello. Along this street **Juliet's house** still stands. It is a romantic thirteenth-century house whose façade is in brick but ennobled by elegant three-lobed windows. Tradition has it that the house belonged to the Capulets. Within the small inner courtyard there is a *bronze statue of Juliet* made by N. Costantini. Above it is the famous *balcony* from which Juliet supposedly looked out to engage in sweet conversation with her beloved. A plaque bears some lines both in English and in Italian translation from this Shakespearean tragedy. Even the inside of the house has been carefully restored to its original fourteenth century appearance.

Romeo and Juliet, a love story

If Verona is considered, along with Terni, the capital of Love, then this is due above all to the immortal story of Romeo Montague and Juliet Capulet. These two young people belong to rival families caught up in a terrible feud. They meet at a masquerade ball, fall in love and realise that in order to see each other they must do it secretly. The strength of their love is such that they even manage to get married, but a cruel destiny seems to be inexorably against their happiness. Tebaldo, Juliet's cousin, has killed Mercutio, one of Romeo's friends. Romeo in turn kills Tebaldo but is then forced to flee from Verona. In the meantime, Juliet tries to defy her father who has already organised a prestigious marriage for her. To get out of this situation, Juliet drinks a potion which makes her seem dead. She does not manage, however, to tell Romeo about this before he steals back into the city. And so the youth, who believes he has lost his beloved Juliet forever, kills himself next to her. Upon awakening, Juliet cannot bear the sight of her beloved's dead body and wills to join him forever in a loving embrace of death. A love which knows no boundaries, no end forces the two feuding families in Shakespeare's tragedy to reconciliation, even though for the two lovers, it is too late. Their love, however, still has a certain power today whereby lots and lots of couples in love send letters to Verona where an authentic Juliet takes the time and care to answer them.

The well-lit elegance of the inner rooms which have been meticulously re-built: the great hall (bottom left) leads to the balcony through a spacious anti-chamber (top left); and the second, third- and fourth-floor rooms of Juliet's house.
It is still possible to admire the refined elegance of the frescoes decorating the walls together with austerely simple furnishings such as the fire-places and wooden stairs.
Top right, the modern decorated ceiling can be seen perfectly blending in with the older structures.

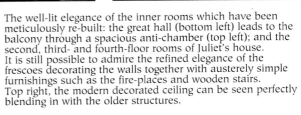

Romeo's house (right) and the empty sarcophagus thought to be the tomb of the unfortunate girl (below) are still today the end of many a pilgrimage embarked upon by lovers of all ages who traditionally leave a written sign of their visit as a token of their feelings in Juliet's house (above).

Romeo's house

Tradition has it that another rather compact fourteenth century house belonged to Romeo and his family, the Montecchi (or Montagues). This house is Gothic in design with a façade in brick and standing in via delle Arche Scaligere. This is obviously a legend inasmuch as historical endeavour has revealed that the so-called **house of Romeo** belonged, rather, to Cagnolo Nogarola. This does not, however, detract from the romantic atmosphere surrounding the building which is articulated around a series of internal courtyards. A certain well-defended look in conferred by the presence of a crown of battlements.

Juliet's tomb

A simple marble sarcophagus lies empty in a crypt in via del Pontiere. It is supported by slabs of stone and probably goes back to the thirteenth or fourteenth century. Today it is considered to have been **Juliet's tomb**. Together with the house which tradition has ascribed to the young girl's family, this tomb is the final destination of a veritable pilgrimage. The crypt housing the sarcophagus was originally part of the *Convent of the Capuchin monks* which makes for a suggestive setting indeed. This is the profoundly Shakespearean atmosphere in which the tomb is immersed and which makes it extremely fascinating.

THE BASILICA OF SAINT ANASTASIA

The **Basilica of Saint Anastasia** is the largest of its kind in Verona. According to some historians, this superb Gothic construction was built by the Dominican Order and dedicated to Saint Peter Martyr, a Dominican monk from Verona and co-patron saint of the city together with Saint Zeno. It is more likely, however, that the Dominicans had actually had it built on the site of an older church previously dedicated to Saint Anastasia.

The building of the Basilica started in 1290 and continued until 1323 but was only really concluded with the work carried out between 1423 and 1481. The church boasts a majestic *apse* in red brick and an extremely high *bell-tower* culminating in a particularly slender spire. The slenderness is conferred by the stone ribbing running around the arris. The façade is also rather austere. Even though the facing was never completely finished in the upper section, the *façade* proudly displays its double-opening ogival *portal* in polychromatic marble. The bas-reliefs with which Ri-gino di Enrico decorated it are taken from the *Stories of the New Testament*, the *Stories of Saint Anastasia*, *Episodes of the Life of Saint Peter Martyr* and the *Stories of the Dominicans*. The basilica also holds by the same artist the *Vergine con Bambino* (Virgin with the Holy Child). The suspended *tomb* in the church is considered by some to be by Guglielmo di Castelbarco, whereas others attribute it to the otherwise unknown "Maestro di Sant'Anastasia". Whichever the case, it is rightly considered to be the forerunner of the famous Della Scala tombs.

The *inside* of the Basilica is divided into a central nave and two side aisles by mighty columns crowned with Gothic capitals. These in turn support the floral decorated vaults. Along the side walls and in the apse 17 *chapels* open up into the church presenting rich collections of noteworthy art works by painters and sculptors from Verona and the Veneto region. Such artists include Girolamo dai Libri, Altichiero and Michele da Firenze whose large works in terracotta

The Basilica di Sant'Anastasia, with its apse and tall bell tower, sits of the bank of the Adige River.

The austere elegant façade of Sant'Anastasia, though incomplete in its upper part, is hallmarked by the timeless fascination conferred by its double portal surrounded by multi-coloured marble and bas-reliefs, and the two slender, agile windows.

present 24 scenes from the *Life of Jesus* (1435). Then there are the creative works by Giovanni di Bartolo, Ranuccio Arvari, Giolfino and even perhaps by Michele Giambono who is tentatively considered to be the author of the imposing *Sepolcro di Cortesia Serego*. Antonio Pisano, as famous as Pisanello but of Veronese origin, painted the large fresco depicting *St. George freeing the Princess* which is a masterpiece of courtly Gothic art. Other works can be ascribed to the skill of Caroto, Liberale (especially his famous *Deposition*), Martino and Stefano da Verona, Brusasorci, Turchi, Bassetti and Rotari.

The extremely famous holy-water fonts of Sant'Anastasia: left, the so-called "fat Hunchback", abovet, the so-called "thin Hunchback". They are taken to represent the workers of the nearby water mills on the Adige River.

Views of the magnificent central nave.

On the wall at the beginning of the right aisle of Sant'Anastasia it is still possible to admire the great work of art by Pisanello dedicated to the legend of St. George.

The 1462 *floor* by Pietro da Porlezza displays extremely refined pictorial taste in its white, pink and grey-blue marble pieces which were also used for the splay of the portal. The two very interesting *holy-water fonts* were sculptured in different times, one at the beginning of the sixteenth century, the other one in 1591. They are curiously supported by two extremely unusual hunchbacks known as the "Hunchbacks of Saint Anastasia" who were probably two workers from the many mills along the nearby Adige river. Outside the church there is the above-mentioned 1320 sarcophagus of Castelbarco who was a powerful feudal lord of the Adige Valley allied with the Della Scala family. In the courtyard of what is now the **Conservatoire**, many other fourteenth-century *tombs* can be admired amongst which the one belonging to Bartolomeo Dussaini.

Bottom and opposite page, the great fresco by Antonio Pisano, called Pisanello, depicting *St. George freeing the Princess*.

The Achille Forti Municipal Gallery of Modern and Contemporary Art

Palazzo Emilei-Forti is an historical building in which Napoleon Bonaparte stayed between 1796 and 1797. Today it has maintained the appearance it had received in the eighteenth century. This, however, was itself a renovation of earlier constructions, including some from the mediaeval period such as the so-called "Palazzo di Ezzelino da Romano." The building underwent further renovation and painstaking restoration under the guidance of Ignazio Pellegrini and in 1937 became the **Achille Forti Municipal Gallery of Modern and Contemporary Art**. Achille Forti was the last member of the noble Forti family and included this project in his will. The Gallery has since become even richer and more prestigious thanks to the organisation of exhibitions and extensive cultural events of international importance. In reality, the gallery has not as yet reached completion. It owns and holds many nineteenth and twentieth-century works, mainly from the area around Verona, such as significant sculptures by Giovanni Dupré, Medardo Rosso and Giacomo Manzù, only to name a few, together with creations by Giovanni Fattori, Filippo De Pisis, Emilio Vedova and Ottone Rosai. The current demise of the Gallery, however, means that only a part of its artistic patrimony can be put on show at any one time. Its beautiful display rooms are already an authentic work of art on their own. The *frescoes* by Francesco Lorenzi, Marco Marcola and Giorgio Anselmi, for example, splendidly embellish the walls. Similarly, the internal *courtyard* holds large Romanesque arches which once constituted the entrance to this beautiful old building.

Angelo Rechia (1816-1882), *Study of artists*. The work is held at the Galleria Comunale d'Arte Moderna e Contemporanea "Achille Forti", housed in the Palazzo Emilei-Forti (above).

THE CATHEDRAL

The *Duomo* or **Cathedral** is dedicated to St. Mary Matricular, just like the earlier basilica which must have been erected in the same area. It is a prestigious example of the most characteristic Veronese Romanesque style. The Cathedral as it stands today dominates a small square resting on the ruins of former churches built in varying eras. The building was consecrated in 1187 but was made taller and enlarged in 1440, as can be gleaned from the *façade* with its large late-Gothic windows embellished by the even later decorative elements. The originally austere Romanesque layout is still richly attested to by the large double *prothyron* protecting the main portal and supported underneath by twisting columns sitting on the back of a couple of winged griffins. Like the prothyron of Zan Zeno, this elegant prothyron is also by Maestro Nicolò, that is, the same architect who planned the entire Romanesque cathedral. He also probably painted in the lunette above the portal in 1138 depicting *Our Lady with Child surrounded by the Magi and shepherds*. Next to *Saints John the Baptist and John the Evangelist*, the same artist also added *hunting scenes*, *prophets* and two *paladins* of the chivalrous Charlemagne cycles, Roland armed with his famous sword and Oliver. This testifies to the development of an elaborate Christian mythology and establishes another analogy with San Zeno. On the right side of the Cathedral there is a door belonging to an earlier construction with a hanging prothyron. There is also the *bell-tower* whose base is thirteenth-century Romanesque and whose central part is sixteenth-century. The last and top-most part was added as late as the twentieth century by the architect E. Fagiuoli. Even today

The Cathedral of Verona with a double storey protyron leading into it. The upper storey is in tufa whereas the lower one frames the portal with a lunette above where an *Our Lady*, an *Announcement to the shepherds* and an *Adoration of the Magi* can be admired.

The magnificent capital of a column of the protyron on the right side of the Cathedral is also well worth noting, evocatively decorated with allegorical figures.

The small yet graceful protyron to be admired on the right side of the Cathedral of Verona (12th century).

Two singular capitals more commonly known as "hunchbacks".

the whole structure is still far from being completely finished. At the back of the Cathedral the outstanding twelfth century *apse* can be admired. The inside is divided into a nave and two aisles. Here Gothic architecture dominates, as can be seen in the strong many-lobed pillars in red marble of Verona and in the pointed arches leading up into the cross cap-vaults in which each of the four sections is painted with golden stars on a blue background. The geometrical flooring is made up of pieces of white, grey-blue and pink marble. Many altars and chapels can be seen elegantly set in fixtures painted by Falconetto in the sixteenth century. The apse basin was frescoed, instead, by il Torbido with the *Annunciation, Episodes from the Life of Mary and*

Prophets taken in the sixteenth century from Giulio Romano's cartoons. Amongst the most noteworthy pictorial works of art in the nave, there is the *Adoration of the Magi* by Liberale da Verona, which was particularly admired by Vasari, the *Deposition with four saints* by Nicolò Giolfino, the eighteenth century *Transfiguration* by Giovan Battista Cignaroli, *Our Lady and Saints Martin and Steven* by il Caroto, the small doors of the organ painted by Brusasorci and *Our Lady of the Assumption* painted in 1535 by Titian. This last painting is later, therefore, than the Venetian one of the Frari, but is perhaps richer in interior humanity. It is held in a frame made by Jacopo Sansovino who also made the *sepulchre for bishop Nichesola* in the chapel by the same name. The fourteenth century *tomb of St. Agata* housed in the Mazzanti Chapel is permeated with charming Gothic elegance. The 1534 semi-circular structure of Ionic columns which surrounds the *choir* of Sanmicheli and closes the presbytery is, instead, classically Renaissance.

A view of the entire structure surrounding the choir closing off the presbytery. Balustrade in multi-coloured marble by Sanmicheli.

The bell tower rising next to the Cathedral. Below: the Chiesa di Sant'Elena, behind an elegant fifteenth century portico.

The Bishopric

The **Tower of Bishop Ognibene** stands above the inner courtyard of the Bishopric and the external walls of the apses of the Church of San Giovanni in Fonte. The tower in question is entirely yellow and endowed with battlements. The structure in tufa was built in 1172, an age in which the residence of the bishop had to be able to carry out defensive functions when necessary. The **Bishopric** which we can admire today proudly displays its sixteenth century appearance. It boasts an interesting portal as its main entrance over which certain *statues of the Virgin, and Saints Peter, Paul and Michael* seem to be guarding. These statues were made by the expert hand of Giovanni da Verona. Noteworthy frescoes by Brusasorci are contained within the palace.

The Church of St. Helen

The ancient quarter surrounding the Cathedral of Verona is one of the most charming areas of the entire city. It is a maze of austere, silent streets running into small squares crowned with imposing private buildings. The **Church of St. Helen** can be found here. It was probably built in the twelfth century but was embellished in the Renaissance with a portico where tradition has it that Dante held his inaugural speech in 1320 *Quaestio de aqua et terra* (The Question of water and earth). Restoration inside has uncovered the ruins of earlier sacred buildings, perhaps an early Christian church of the ninth century. Certain paintings can be admired hanging on the walls, such as the interesting *Stations of the Cross* probably painted before the fourteenth century and a painting by Brusasorci depicting *Our Lady with St. Helen and St. George.*

In front of the Chiesa di Sant'Elena one of the true jewels of Veronese Romanesque architecture opens out, the Chapter Cloister, built in the twelfth century and partially re-built after 1945. It is articulated by a long series of small columns which, on the eastern side, stand in two orders of arches. The fifteenth century well still stands in the centre. The Chapter Library, perhaps the oldest in all of Europe, looks out on to this cloister.

The Chapter Cloister and Library

In the immediate vicinity of the Cathedral one of Verona's most beautiful cloisters can be found, the **Chapter Cloister**. It was built in 1140 above the ruins of the early Christian basilica. Its elegant and extremely pure Romanesque style can be admired in the small columns arranged in couples which, on the eastern side, pan out into a double order of small arches. The walls of the cloister contain some noteworthy *mosaics* made for the two basilicas built in the days of St. Zeno. There are still other mosaics which are hidden, however, by the lawn within the cloister.

The **Chapter Library** faces the cloister but there is also another entrance from the Piazza del Duomo (the Cathedral Square). This is probably the oldest library in all of Europe. It came into being in the fifth century as the natural descendant of the busy Roman *scriptoria* where the canonical members of the Cathedral could also study. Petrarch is said to have looked through these treasures searching for lost manuscripts. Indeed, many precious texts from the fifth and sixth centuries are still kept here, such as the *Institutiones* of Caius (fifth century) and the famous *Codex Justinianeus* (sixth century). There are also more than 11,000 manuscripts many of which are illuminated, incunabula and ancient works of art such as the bust of Homer (third century BC). A visit would not be complete without admiring the astonishing wealth of the small but fascinating **Museo Canonicale** which houses paintings and sculptures from the twelfth century.

The Church of San Giovanni in Fonte
(Cathedral Baptistery)

San Giovanni in Fonte was originally the cathedral baptistery. Its current form goes back to 1123 when it was rebuilt after the 1117 earthquake, on the ruins of the eighth-ninth century baptistery. It is in tufa and its nave is longer than its two aisles. Its elegant apses face the courtyard of the Bishopric.

On the inside, the columns still support the original capitals from the prior phases of building whereas the walls bear frescoes which were made between the thirteenth and fifteenth centuries. They also carry paintings by Paolo Farinati, Giovanni Caroto e Falconetto.

By far the most precious treasure, however, held in San Giovanni in Fonte is the monolithic *baptismal font* circa thirteenth century. Its octagonal form and the Veronese marble from which it was hewn give it a similar appearance to thé font in San Zeno. It can well be considered one of the loftiest heights of Veronese art of its time, especially because of its extraordinary naturalistic vivacity and the elegant plasticity of the bas-reliefs decorating it. These include the panels separated by spiralling pilaster strips: the *Annunciation*, the *Visit to Mary*, the *Birth of Jesus*, the *Announcement to the shepherds*, the *Adoration of the Magi*, *Herod ordering the massacre of the innocent*, the *Flight to Egypt*, the *Baptism of Jesus*. These are thought to be the works of two artists, one Briolato, who also made the Wheel of Fortune in San Zeno, and another excellent sculptor of a more characteristic Venetian and Byzantine style.

Inside the Chiesa di San Giovanni in Fonte there is still the magnificent, octagonal baptismal font. It is decorated with splendid bas-reliefs which make this one of the masterpieces of fourteenth century sculpture in Verona.

The Stone Bridge is protected by the thirteenth century Guard Bridge. It still preserves today its most ancient arches of Roman origin shown on the right. The rest is built of brick strengthened by stone. It was painstakingly re-built altogether after the war during which it had been destroyed by the retreating Germans.

With its asymmetrical structure and the profile of a donkey's back crossing the Adige River, the Stone Bridge has become a true symbol of the city.

Il Ponte Pietra

As far as we know, only two bridges crossed the Adige River in Roman times, the *Postumius* and the *Marmoreus*. The *Postumius* went from the end of the great *decumanus* whereas the *Marmoreus* had been built slightly farther up hill near the great bend in the river. The *Pons Postumius* was so-called from the name of the road which crossed it and then ran through the city and along the left bank of the Adige River. By the tenth century the documents already mention it as the "broken bridge". The floods of 1154 and 1239 brought about the complete disappearance of the bridge.

The plight of the *Pons Marmoreus* has been quite different. Radical transformation has given it the name of **Ponte Pietra** (the Stone Bridge). Little remains of the ancient Roman bridge except for the barely visible stone ashlars corresponding to the two large archways closest to the left bank of the river. Devastating floods and extensive damage, with the consequent attempts at restoration, have altered the structure giving it quite an irregular appearance. Its dramatic arching form with the five asymmetrical archways underneath respect the current of the Adige river. Because of the rather sharp bend in the river itself, the current flows more quickly towards the left bank. Here the river has been strengthened in a somewhat rustic fashion. It rests on four stone "bows" built to slice through the current which is at its strongest. The bridge has always been one of the city's symbolic monuments with reproductions of it appearing in the works of artists ever since the fifteenth century. Its name, however, does not really describe its true nature. Only the

first two archways on the left are in white stone and are obviously Roman. The other three were rebuilt with bricks in the sixteenth century with only the profiles and piers lined with stone. Quite unabashedly, however, one might argue that in the very same eclectic construction lies its fascination. The end result is evocative and picturesque, especially in its chromatic patterns of reds and whites brought together with ingeniousness and unpredictability. The spectacularly romantic construction thus fuses together the classical Roman era with the lavish simplicity of mediaeval Romanesque. The *Torre di Guardia* (Watch Tower) was fittingly built by Alberto I della Scala in the thirteenth century to defend the entrance onto the bridge. Its great "eye" discharging the flood waters and the parapet bordered by a double strip of white stone supported by an uninterrupted series of shelves were then added in the sixteenth century.

The most recent damage caused to the bridge occurred during the Second World War when it, together with the other bridges of Verona, was blown up by the withdrawing German troops.

The Soprintendenza ai Monumenti (government department responsible for monuments and other artistic treasures) had fortunately foreseen the event and had already had the bridge photographed with every detail of the bridge documented. After the war it was therefore possible, though painstakingly difficult, to find and number all the fragments. This allowed for a full restoration of the bridge. Today it is no longer possible to see that the bridge had undergone such violence.

The Roman Theatre

The centre of the Roman city was situated very near Ponte Pietra. Here, on the side of the hill, then-called Mons Gallus, but now known as Castel San Pietro, the fan-like structure of the **Roman theatre** can be admired. Its primitive structure can be dated back to the first century BC under Augustus. The very first permanent stone theatre in Rome had been built by Pompeius only a few decades beforehand. The growing importance of Verona within the Roman State can be inferred from this. Verona's theatre, together with the one built in Trieste a little later, is one of the largest and best conserved in the *X Regio Venetia et Histria*, the territorial district to which the city belonged.

Unlike the Amphitheatre, this Roman theatre has suffered bad damage over the centuries from earthquakes, flooding, time and man. Gradually the ancient centre of entertainment was covered over by ruins and almost buried under new buildings. Theodoric's palace seems to have been built here before giving way to the building for the Longobard kings and their successors.

Any number of churches, convents and huts would then surround them. Despite the flourishing of these urban superstructures, the memory of the theatre lived on down through the centuries with names such as "labyrinth", "grottos", etc, where hermits, monks, confraternities and artists would go to live.

The first excavations meant to bring the theatre back to life were carried out in 1757 thanks to the abbot Fontana. In 1830 the archaeologist, Andrea Monga, bought all the houses on the hill and had them demolished. He, however, died shortly afterwards. Work resumed in 1905 and continued until 1912. They started again in 1939 but were only really finished in 1955. Today the theatre is 109x138 m against the original 123x152 m. Its axes are 43 and 73 m long.

Like all Roman buildings of this type, Verona's theatre has a semicircular *cavea* (horseshoe shaped auditorium) with tiers. The stage is closed off by the fixed wall at the back and an area for the orchestra otherwise used for the most distinguished guests. The overall technique is a mix of Greek and Roman architecture. The central cavea lays its tiers onto the hollowed

The characteristic half-circle of the large Roman Theatre opens out on to the banks of the Adige River, at the foot of the hill of Castel San Pietro.

out side of the hill while the lateral cavea is completely Roman in style whose brick work is the same as that in the Arena. So as to prevent the seepage of water from within the hill into the cavea and tiers, the ingenious, able builders realised that they should partially isolate the theatre from the hill, which they did by leaving a large, deep gap between the theatre itself and the tufa underneath.

Despite its being two thousand years old, thanks to the skill and craftsmanship of its planners and builders, the magnificent Roman Theatre still carries out its original function. Like the Arena, the Roman Theatre is a place for theatrical entertainment. Since 1948 prose, ballets and concerts of international acclaim have been held here. These go from the *Shakespearean Festival* to the theatre of Goldoni, no less prestigious in the Veneto.

Two other buildings here add to the atmosphere. These are the **Convento di San Girolamo** (St. Jerome Convent), which is now the *Museo Archeologico*, and the **Chiesa dei Santi Siro e Libera** (Church of St. Sirus and St. Libera). These were added in the course of the centuries to the side of the hill and theatre. The Church in question was built in the tenth century but was profoundly modified in the sixteenth and seventeenth centuries, as can be gleaned by the double *staircase* of the Baroque period. The Church dominates the eastern side of the theatre's tiers. It also houses a noteworthy eighteenth century *grand altar*, a wooden *choir* attributed to the eighteenth century German artists Kraft, Petendorf and Siut, not to mention various other pieces such as a *Madonna e San Gaetano* by G. Cignaroli (1751) and an *Annunciazione* by Ridolfi.

The seats are on the whole well preserved. They curiously descend from the steps of the Baroque Church of St. Sirus and St. Libera.

The Archaeological Museum

The **Museo Archeologico** houses many of the most salient artistic treasures of Roman Verona. The museum itself is in the very heart of Verona's archaeological site, that is, in the austere rooms of the former *Convento di San Girolamo*. Here interesting collections of ceramics, bronze pieces and sculptures can be admired, for example, a statuette of *Tiberius*, a double-headed *herma*, many Roman copies of Greek originals, the *Head of a leading member of the Julius-Claudia family* (first century AD) together with altars, stele and various funeral monuments. The Roman *mosaics* deserve special attention, especially the first century AD *Clash of the Gladiators*. Amongst the cloisters and *Nymphaeum*, which is an interesting Roman creation hewn out of the rock of the hill, the former grandeur of the **Chiesa di San Girolamo** can easily be inferred. Its early Christian floor, for example, is still intact, as are the noteworthy *frescoes* amongst which the *Annunciazione* by Caroto carried out in 1508. Above the altar there is a fifteenth century *triptych* accompanied by a fourth-century sculpture of the *Good Shepherd*.

The Church of St. Steven

Not far from Ponte Pietra, the **Church of St. Steven the protomartyr** can be found. A local tradition places it as the Cathedral of Verona between 412 and 750. More probably it was, however, a simple oratory for several centuries perhaps destroyed by Theodoric and then re-built. The first bishops of the city were nevertheless buried here, but this was only due to the fact that Roman law imposed burial outside the city walls where this church, in fact, stood. After the devastating earthquake of 1117, the church was rebuilt over the ruins of the earlier church. The resulting basilica stands as an example of the renewed vigour in building characteristic of the new millennium. The plan was based on the Latin cross but during the course of the fourteenth century the apse was extended and embellished with an octagonal lantern in brick made to look lighter by two tiers of mullioned windows of Lombard origin. The tufa and brick *façade* is surrounded by strong buttresses and made elegant by the blind arches under the eaves. On the inside, the nave and two aisles are divided by somewhat roughly hewn, square pillars in stone. The overall effect is of great, typically mediaeval simplicity dominated by the presbytery placed at the top of a central staircase under which the crypt can be found. It is exactly the presbytery in *Santo Stefano*, together with the lantern, which introduces a particular stylistic variation into the local Romanesque style. The main altar is surrounded by a semi-circular gallery which is a sort of ambulatory with a vaulted ceiling supported by columns and capitals which are the last remaining constitutive elements of the eighth century church. Here the *bishop's throne* is to be found. The *crypt* is mystical and dark and follows the plan of the gallery above whereby eighth century columns and capitals create a particularly evocative atmosphere. In the nave a polychromatic fourteenth century statue dominates. It represents *St. Peter on his throne* holding his keys which are a symbol of his divine power. The medal on his chest depicts St. Peter being liberated from prison. This fine piece of sculpture was made by Rigino di Enrico. The statue once proudly stood in the Church of St. Peter in Castello which no longer exists. Two frescoes of the Veronese Gothic school and datable in the fourteenth and fifteenth centuries, have been attributed to Martino da Verona. They depict the *Incoronation of the Virgin* and the *Annunciation*. A touching *Our Lady breast-feeding* of the late fourteenth century is thought, instead, to be the work of Giacomo da Riva. Among such rigour of form and image, one can also surprisingly find the fascinating baroque *Chapel of the Innocent*. It is so called because local tradition believed that some of the babies King Herod had massacred had been buried here. It was actually built, rather, to house between 1619 and 1621 the mortal remains of certain martyrs and bishops of the city.

The simple yet elegant façade of the Church of St. Steven the protomartyr is one of the most ancient in Verona. It is made of tufa and brick. The blind arch motif running under the eaves, together with its linear and quite austere architectural structure, still allows us to glean the full thrust of the austere fascination of an early Christian basilica.

Not far from the Lungadige San Giorgio stands San Giorgio in Braida. This is an eleventh-century Benedictine monastery.

This gate opens up on Via Postumia and was the main gate to the city of Verona in Roman times. It took its name from the personnel collecting taxes for the bishop.

San Giorgio in Braida

Not far from the Austrian fortifications near the Lungadige San Giorgio stands **San Giorgio in Braida**. This is an eleventh-century Benedictine monastery which passed over, in 1442, to the congregation of San Giorgio in Alga. In the second half of the fifteenth century the entire complex underwent radical transformation which was to give it the appearance it has today. Furthermore, a century later, Sanmicheli's project for the new presbytery, dome and tambour required that the original Romanesque tower be sacrificed. The elegant marble *façade* dates back to the end of the sixteenth century. The *statues* to be admired in its niches represent *Saint George* and *Saint Lorenzo Giustiniani* by Giacomo Ceola and Lorenzo Muttoni. Even though it was probably Sanmicheli who designed the *bell-tower*, it was Bernardino Brugnoli who executed it. He, however, never finished it.
The *inside* of the church has no side aisles and shows obvious signs of work carried out by Sanmicheli, such as in the structure of the four chapels opening in each side and in the holy-water fonts in marble preserved there. There are also works by other artists ennobling the church. These include the *Martyrdom of Saint George* decorating the high altar reminiscent in style of works by Sanmicheli. It is an authentic masterpiece by Paolo Veronese. There is also *Our Lady in glory and the three Arcangels* by Felice Brusasorci, the *Annunciation* by Giovanni Caroto framing the triumphal arch of the presbytery, *Our Lady sitting on her throne with Baby Jesus between Saints Zeno and Lorenzo Giustiniani* by Girolamo dai Libri, the *Baptism of Jesus* by Jacopo Tintoretto on the counter-façade and *Our Lady appearing to Saints Cecily, Agnes, Barbara, Lucy and Catherine* by Moretto da Brescia. The rectory built up against the church in 1791 by Luigi Trezza is very interesting. On its façade there still remain the signs of the warfare which occurred between the French and the Austrians 18 October 1805.

La Porta dei Borsari

La **Porta dei Borsari** (the "Borsari" Gate) opens to the south of the first city wall at the beginning of the Great Decumanus and at the end of the main street by the same name. For two thousand years it has regulated intense traffic into the city. Originally it only constituted the outer part of a building no longer standing today but which, then, had been built into the city walls in order to fortify them and to house those guarding the main entrance into the city. Its current name, however, is mediaeval, going back to the period in which the customs officers placed high tolls on all merchandise being brought into or out of the city. The customs duty, locally called the "toloneo", was imposed by the bishop and canons of the Cathedral. The large bags (borse) which the customs officers wore gave rise to the term "Borsari" and then to a new name for the gate itself. The gate was part of the city quarter dedicated to the patron saint of Verona, Saint Zeno, whose church stood here.
The Gate was made in the first century AD of white stone from the Valpolicella quarries. Its characteristics are typical of early imperial architecture. The lowest part of the three tiered structure opened out into two rounded archways flanked by fluted semicolumns crowned with Corinthian capitals supporting the two architraves and tympanum. The two tiers above hold six arched windows separated by columns and pillars which support architraves both with and without a tympanum.
Originally the gate must have been flanked by two cylindrical *towers* whose ruins have been found in the houses on both sides.

Corso Cavour

One of the most famous and elegant streets in the city of Verona is **Corso Cavour** which substantially runs along what was the suburban section of the ancient Via Postumia. Corso Cavour starts from the Porta dei Borsari and opens out further along into a small square. Some of Verona's finest buildings can be seen along Corso Cavour. For example, the *Casa dei Giolfino* (House of the Giolfino Family), which faces the small square in Corso Cavour, was once the residence of this interesting family of artists. The building is more commonly known now for the frescoes in its façade, such as *Knights duelling* and *Condottiero on his horse*, both by Nicolò Giolfino. During the Middle Ages this street had become an important city axis not only for the suburban population around it but also for the running of Verona's *palio*. It was, however, during the course of the sixteenth century that this same axis developed into a prestigious residential area. The beautiful **Palazzo Bevilacqua**, for example, was built in the sixteenth century, together with the large **Palazzo Canossa** with its unmistakable covering in ashlar-work, designed and partially built by Sanmicheli between 1530 and 1537. It would only be truly completed a century later by Lelio and Vincenzo Pellesina. There is also **Palazzo Carnesali** together with the slightly older **Palazzo Medici** in front of Piazza Santi Apostoli and **Palazzo Scannagatti** which, though Renaissance in design, was radically altered during the nineteenth century. Only in 1665 was the very ostentatious **Palazzo Carlotti** then added by Prospero Schiavi who built it with three orders of sculptured windows.

The entrance with three barrel-vaults of Palazzo Canossa by Sanmicheli covered with its characteristic smooth ashlar-work.

Interesting views of the Roman pavement in excellent state of conservation. It was unearthed during the road works on Corso Cavour. The careful choice of the stone and the way they all fit perfectly together can easily be seen.

THE ARCO DEI GAVI

At first glance this seems to be a classical arch of triumph with its one barrel-vault mounted by a tympanum. It is, instead, a monument built in the first century AD to celebrate one of the most conspicuous families in Roman Verona, the gens Gauia. The names of some of the components of this family can still be read today under the niches which housed the statues to them. These were Strabo, Maximus, Macro, Lucius and Vibius. On the inside of the building another inscription is to be found: "L[ucius] Vitruvius L[ibertus] Cerdo Architectus". This is the name of the man who built it which means that this is the only "autographed" Roman building in the entire city. The position of this building is one of privilege inasmuch as it marked the beginning of the *Via Sacra*. This was a straight road lined with tombs where the Via Postumia made its entrance into Verona. In time, however, the arch was to gradually lose its celebratory function and splendour until it eventually became part of the communal walls with the name of *Nuova Porta di San Zeno* (St. Zeno's New Gate). Next to it Castelvecchio was developed together with the huge Torre dell'Orologio (Clock Tower). Despite its decline, however, the ancient **Arco dei Gavi** continued to be admired throughout the Renaissance for its elegance and rigour in architectural design. It thus became a model for masters such as Iacopo Bellini, Mantegna, Falconetto, Antonio da Sangallo, Palladio, Sanmicheli and Caroto. Destiny was, however, to prove fatal under Napoleon. In 1805 the Arch was taken down because it obstructed military traffic. Eugene, Napoleone's viceroy for Verona, was sorry about the demolition and decided to make a large sum of money available for the Municipality of Verona to rebuild the

Large and monumental, the Arch of the Gavi family is known to be one of the rare examples of Roman arches of triumph dedicated to a private family.

monument at a later time. The fragments were therefore numbered and stored in safety. Not only was the work of rebuilding it to take place more than a century later in 1932, but it was also carried out on a different site. The small square in front of Castelvecchio was chosen, on the banks of the Adige River, where the viceroy's money, which had been deposited in a local bank, contributed to its rebuilding.

A segment of ancient Roman paving still perfectly intact in the shadow of the arch.

The Church of St. Lawrence

The **Church of St. Lawrence** now looks onto Corso Cavour. As an early Christian basilica, however, in the eighth century it actually rose outside the Roman walls of the city. To enter the side courtyard it is still necessary, in fact, to pass underneath the fifteenth century Gothic archway, still crowned with a statue of St. Lawrence, and leave the Porta dei Borsari behind. Though no longer fully original with its fifteenth century bell-tower and Renaissance protyron to the side, the Church of St. Lawrence still remains a remarkably interesting example of Romanesque architecture. There are Byzantine and Norman elements in the *matronea* or loggias half-way up the nave walls provided for the women and the *small cylindrical towers* on the façade which support two winding staircases leading up to the same *matronea*.

The *nave* is very tall and slender, like the aisles, and completely built in tufa and brick. Painting and perspective confer the impression of even greater height. The light filters in through the small splayed windows to dissolve the semi-shadow within. The structure as it stands today goes back to the first decades of the twelfth century. Brickwork in river-stone and brick, together with traces of thirteenth century fresco work, confirm the historical importance of this Christian temple which is considered one of the most interesting examples of Veronese Romanesque today. Inside there are also works of art such as the painting by Domenico Brusasorci depicting the *Virgin and St. Lawrence, St. John the Baptist and St. Augustine* and the austere sixteenth century funeral monuments of the Nogarolas and Romana Trivella.

The very ancient Chiesa di San Lorenzo still holds the fascination of its early Christian and Romanesque origins in its nave, aisles and matronea. The façade is particularly interesting, closed in, as it is, between two cylindrical towers. The tombs of Nogarola and Romana Trivella go back to the 16th century.

CASTELVECCHIO

The appearance today of **Castelvecchio** is indeed quite different to its original state. The huge manor house with a mighty crenellated bridge was built by the Della Scala in the fourteenth century. Francesco Bevilacqua, captain of the Della Scala family, placed the first stone in 1355 by order of Cangrande II. This act is recorded in a plaque in one of the courtyards. The grandiose structure, however, seems to have been built to defend the family from internal enemies rather than from any outside attack. This indeed is a characteristic of many castles built in the same period during which the power of any ruling dynasty was never completely secured. Castelvecchio, then, in order to carry out its functions of defence and war as well as possible, was built as a compact structure out of solid and uniformly red bricks. No thought was given to the more refined touches of Gothic architecture. The main aim was to confer strength. Courtyards, towers and passageways intersect and cross each other over communal walls and Roman fragments. Indeed, a good section of the older communal walls, which ran right down to the river, was included to as to strengthen further the new building. Its original name was San Martino al Ponte because the castle was built on an older site with a tiny *church* dedicated to St. Martin adjacent to the bridge over the Adige River. Recent excavation has rediscovered this tiny church together with the ancient *Postierla del Morbio*. The castle was called "vecchio" (old) because only a few decades after its being finished, the Visconti family built a new castle on Colle di San Pietro together with a fortress called San Felice. Castelvecchio in turn was to be successively modified by future invaders such as the Venetians, the French and the Austrians. It thus became barracks, an arsenal and a jail, all of which left indelible signs in its structure. For example, several towers and battlements were knocked down, only to be re-built in the middle

The mighty structures of Castelvecchio and its crenellated bridge, as seen from the Adige River.

The covered towers, the mighty ramparts, which were re-built only during the twentieth century, and the walls which are double and parallel in certain segments and include the old Communal walls of the city in others, underline the primary defensive role of the fortress carried out by Castelvecchio.
This role was carried out on the inside as well.

of the twentieth century. Today six covered *towers* set out the incredibly irregular fortified perimeter. Around it flow the waters of the Adigetto in a deep parallel moat. The powerful *Mastio*, the highest and heaviest tower, dominates the entire building and holds guard over the three inner courtyards. This is where Napoleon had the *fortino* (tiny fort) built, which can still be visited today. During the early part of the Twentieth century, in its very own halls the old castle witnessed the court case of Galeazzo Ciano and some of the atrocities perpetrated by the protagonists of the Republic of Salò. Castelvecchio was seriously damaged during the Second World War. It was later the object of several rebuilding projects which restored it to its original, imposing splendour. Today Castelvecchio is the prestigious seat of the **Museo Civico** by the same name.

The wide, spacious courtyard which opens up inside the eastern-most part of Castelvecchio is surrounded by solid walls dominated in turn by mighty towers. It is, however, softened, in what was the parade-ground of the barracks, by a quiet little garden. Next to what was the draw-bridge of the old fortress, the wing running parallel to the Adige River now houses the Museo Civico.

The Museo Civico di Castelvecchio

The superb structure of Castelvecchio houses one of the most interesting art collections not in Italy but in the whole of Europe - the **Museo Civico di Castelvecchio**. The museum is currently set out in a functional yet picturesque fashion. The rigorous restoration started in 1957 sought to return the monumental structure as much as possible to its original appearance. Prior to this there had already been radical restoration done in 1923 after it had been decided that Castelvecchio should become the seat of the new museum project. Its various *rooms* set out on two floors are dedicated to individual artistic sectors; for example, the *room of Venetian Romanesque sculpture* houses fine works of the twelfth and thirteenth centuries such as the *Arca dei Santi Sergio e Bacco*, a bas-relief sculpture made in 1179; the *rooms of fourteenth century sculpture from Verona* house the *statues of Santa Caterina and Santa Cecilia* together with an expressive *Crucifixion* from the church of San Giacomo di Tomba. The Crucifixion in question was made in tufa at

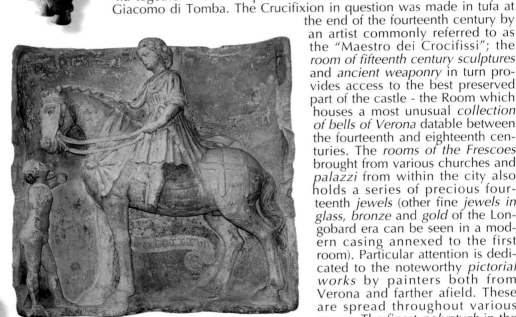

the end of the fourteenth century by an artist commonly referred to as the "Maestro dei Crocifissi"; the *room of fifteenth century sculptures* and *ancient weaponry* in turn provides access to the best preserved part of the castle - the Room which houses a most unusual *collection of bells of Verona* datable between the fourteenth and eighteenth centuries. The *rooms of the Frescoes* brought from various churches and *palazzi* from within the city also holds a series of precious fourteenth *jewels* (other fine *jewels in glass*, *bronze* and *gold* of the Longobard era can be seen in a modern casing annexed to the first room). Particular attention is dedicated to the noteworthy *pictorial works* by painters both from Verona and farther afield. These are spread throughout various rooms. The finest *polyptych* in the collection is the one of the school of Altichiero. Next to the polyptychs and antependia, famous paintings can be admired by masters of the International Gothic movement, such as the lovely *Madonna della Quaglia* (Our Lady of the Quail) by Pisanello and the *Vergine col Bambino* (Virgin with Child) and the *Madonna del Roseto* (Our Lady of the Rose garden) both attributed to the hand of Stefano da Verona. Jacopo Bellini is also well represented, especially in his *Madonna dell'Umiltà* (Our Lady of Humility) and *San Girolamo* (St. Jerome). Mantegna's presence is particularly significant inasmuch as he profoundly influenced painting in the entire Venetian area. There are works by him such as the famous *Sacra Famiglia*

Among the rich, multifarious collections constituting the inestimable patrimony of the Museo Civico in Castelvecchio, there is an extremely interesting collection of works of religious art including sculptures, paintings, works in relief and illuminated manuscripts. These come chiefly from Verona but also include works from other geographical areas both in Italy and abroad.

Following pages: Two famous works held at the Museo Civico of Castelvecchio; Stefano da Verona (1374 ca. – 1450 ca.) *Our Lady of the Rose Garden* and *Our Lady of the Quail*, attributed to Pisanello (15th century).

Art treasures held in Museo Civico of Castelvecchio:
above, *Salome holding the Baptist's head*, by
Callisto Piazza (1500-1562); and *Portrait of Girolamo
Savonarola*, by Alessandro Bonvicino (1498-1554);
below, *A country concert*, by Tintoretto (1518-1594).

The Deposition by Paolo Veronese
(1528-1588).

Portrait of Pase Guarienti in military dress,
attributed to Paolo Veronese.

(Holy Family) and *Cristo Portacroce* (Christ bearing the Cross).
The museum also holds works by less well-known artists such
as Niccolò di Pietro Gerini, Liberale da Verona, Giambono,
Giovanni Bellini, Vittore Carpaccio, Francesco Morone, Fran-
cesco Bonsignori, Caroto, Carlo Crivelli, Girolamo dai Libri.
Moving into the sixteenth, seventeenth and eighteenth cen-
turies, there are the extremely well-known painters such as
Paolo Veronese (*Deposizione*), Tintoretto (*Pala Bevilacqua*),
Sebastiano del Piombo, Lorenzo Lotto, Bernardo Strozzi,
Francesco Guardi and Giovan Battista Tiepolo. A room has
been especially set aside for illustrious foreign painters such as
Van Cleef, Jordaens and Rubens.
A special mention must also be made for an area adjacent to
the Mastio where *ancient weaponry* and *cloth* from the sepulchre in Santa Maria Antica of Cangrande I della Scala are on
display. During the thirteenth century an extraordinary *equestrian statue* of this prince was made to crown his tomb. The
original can be seen today in the heart of the museum whereas a faithful copy was made for and placed back on the
sepulchre.

Right:
Domestic scene with family,
by Pietro Longhi
(1702-1785).

Below: *St. Thomas doubting,*
by Paolo Morando
(1486-1522).

Left: *Pia dei Tolomei led to the Maremma*, by Pompeo Molmenti (1819-1894).

Below: *A kitchen*, by Marten van Cleef (1527-1581).

The Ponte Scaligero

This **bridge** built by the Della Scala family connects the fortified Castelvecchio to the left bank of the Adige River. It represents an almost unique example of a fortified mediaeval bridge built of brick and endowed with towers, battlements and passageways. It was obviously built for defence. It is almost like an extension of the castle built over the mighty Adige River. The largest of its three asymmetrical arches has a 48 m wide opening. It was seriously damaged by the withdrawing German troops in 1945 but was perfectly restored with its original materials.

The mighty Della Scala Bridge (Ponte Scaligero)
is an integral structure in the fortress. It crosses the
Adige River from the large Mastio and the
Porta del Morbio. Three arches comprise its breath
with strong crenellated towers. The crenallation is a
constant feature of the entire bridge, being, at it is,
a continuation of the battlements
characterising the fortress.

THE BASILICA OF SAINT ZENO

Together with the Arena, this **basilica** can well be considered the most important building in the city. Despite this, at the beginning of the nineteenth century masses were not celebrated in it for a long time so it was consequently abandoned altogether. An early church was originally built on the same site between the fourth and fifth centuries. The construction of another one was ordered by the king of the Franks, Pipin, and the bishop Ratholdus. It was probably in this second church that the body of Saint Zeno was solemnly entombed in 807. Down through the following centuries the basilica underwent enlargement, rebuilding and destruction by earthquake and invasion. After a particularly violent seismic event, it was restored in 1120 when it was radically renewed and enlarged. It seems that the bell-tower was added in this phase, that is, around 1045. The renovation work seems to have continued until almost the fourteenth century. Indeed, the apse we can admire today was built between 1386 and 1398. Its style is Gothic with a hull-like ceiling. At the same time, next to the basilica, a large Benedictine **abbey** was being built. It is mentioned by Dante in *Purgatory* and was elected as a favourite place to stay by emperors such as Otto I, Fredrick I "Barbarossa" and Frederick II. Today the only parts remaining of this once mighty building are the imposing *tower* crowned with Ghibelline battlements and the *rooms of the rectory*. The *façade* of the basilica is large and yet unassuming. It is built is tufa and marble with its central part much taller than the two lateral parts. Pilasters and thin pilaster strips confer an idea of thin verticality whereas the chiaroscuro of the small loggia with double arches in marble adds pictorial elegance. The circular rose window makes the façade seems lighter still and is reminiscent of the fickleness of luck, known otherwise as the *Wheel of Fortune*. This splendid window is the work of the sculptor Brioloto for whom there are documents datable between 1189 and 1220. Brioloto sculptured six human figures in various positions each representing particularly happy moments of life. It

The splendid Basilica di San Zeno Maggiore, flanked on the right by a lofty bell tower and on the left by the crenellated tower which once belonged to the no longer existent Abbey of San Zeno.

seems that Brioloto is responsible for the entire façade whereas the friezes, hunting scenes and decorations seem to be attributable to Adamino da San Giorgio who was a sculptor working in 1225 and very probably originally from Valpolicella. The *portal* is unusually rich in sculptured decoration. It is framed by a tall *prothyron* supported by columns resting on lions made in marble from Verona. This was created, so it seems, by a certain Nicolò around 1138, that is, before the construction of the other parts of the façade. It is likely to have been inserted during one of the many phases of rebuilding. It is decorated with the figures of *Saints John the Evangelist* and *John the Baptist*, not to mention representations of the twelve *Months*. On the sides of the prothyron there are two series of bas-relief sculptures telling the *stories of Genesis* and the *Gospel*. They curiously parallel from above episodes taken from mediaeval tales of knights and popular stories, such as the *Duel between Theodoric and Odovacer*, *Theodoric hunting a stag in hell*. And somewhere between these stories inspired by faith and chivalry, there is also the story of a mysterious woman by the name of *Mataliana*. All these sculptures seem to be attributable to the work of Guglielmo and Nicolò and their helpers. Proudly standing out in the middle of the lunette there is *Saint Zeno amongst foot soldiers and knights*. The monumental *door* is decked in 48 bronze panels. The oldest ones go back to the beginning of the twelfth century and are the work of Germanic creativity. The last ones, instead, were added at the end of the thirteenth century and display the purest forms of Italian art of the period. The entire work was composed by several different authors. The themes are taken from both the Old and New Testaments with the addition of four miracles performed by Saint Zeno. Each single panel and the group they collectively make up are framed by the presence of animal heads, allegorical figures, figures of saints and the remarkable representation of a man in the act of sculpting-most certainly one of the creators of this work. The group is one of the most expressive documents of mediaeval Italian sculpture. The

On this page, the two lions supporting the columns of the protryon and a view of the bas-reliefs to be admired on the left of the wooden door which protects the main door behind. It is embellished with bronze plates.

Opposite page: details of the large sculptured rose window, known also as the "Wheel of Fortune", together with decorative elements characterising the refined protyron on the façade of San Zeno.

A complete view of the protyron underlining the extreme elegance of the refined decorative apparatus framing it.

lofty, splendid *bell-tower* proudly stands on the lawn in front of the basilica. One of the three bells placed there in 1149 can still be heard. This bell has an octagonal form and is called, for reasons which still remain unknown, *del figàr*. It might even have been placed on the first bell-tower finished in 1067, in which case it would be the oldest bell in the entire territory around Verona. Between the church and the bell-tower a white Roman *sarcophagus* can be seen lying on the grass. As the Latin inscription points out, the sarcophagus is said to have been the tomb of king Pipin. There is, however, no sound historical justification to believe it. Down through the

centuries, the basilica has undergone relatively few structural changes on the inside and even these have been almost irrelevant. The nave and two aisles of the so-called parish church come together in the elevated presbytery, otherwise called the upper church. This can be reached by climbing one of the side stair cases. The apse behind it, designed by Giovanni and Nicolò da Ferrara in the fourteenth century, is polygonal and Gothic in form. Mighty pillars alternate with the columns to hold up the lofty vaults and two transversal round arches crossing the nave. There are also other plastic elements well worth attention: the twelfth-century *baptismal font* hewn out of a monolithic block of marble from Verona, two *holy-water fonts*, the second altar of the right, groups of columns resting on the lion of Saint Mark and the ox of Saint Luke with serpents winding around them. The *statues of Christ and the Apostles* are held to be by an artist from Verona working in the thirteenth century. They are lined up on the balustrade which separates the area of the presbytery from the nave below. These statues are terribly solemn and most severe in expression when compared to the huge image of *Saint Zeno* who is shown to be cheerful as he blesses the faithful from the left apsidiole. He is holding his pastoral staff with which he has caught a silver trout. This depiction of Saint Zeno was made in polychromatic marble and is particularly dear to the people of Verona. Saint Proculus was a bishop from Verona in the early Christian era. He is represented in a *statue* placed next to the sacristy. The statue in question bears the signature of Giovanni Rigino who was one of the masters of sculpture in fourteenth century Verona. By going down into the crypt sculptured polychromatic decorations can be seen in the vaults between the seven wide arches. The decorations include scenes of hunting after fantastic imaginary animals and stylised floral patterns. The two arches to the right bear the signature of Adamino da San Giorgio. The *crypt* is rather spacious. It has in fact been divided into nine different sectors by a true-to-life wood of columns culminating in capitals of varying eras and styles. The tall pillars and columns standing in the presbytery rest precisely on these strong foundations. Here the *sarcophagus of Saints Lucillus, Lupicillus and Crescentianus* can be found. It is widely believed to be twelfth-century but

The magnificent door composed on bronze plates in which, via obvious reference to the relief work of the protyron, illustrate *stories from the Old and New Testaments*, together with *episodes from the life of St. Zeno* and other figures such as *saints* and crowned *kings*.

Saint Zeno

Zeno was of African origin. The dark complexion of his skin won him the nickname of "Il Moro" (the Moor or "dark-one"). Zeno lived in the fourth century AD and was created bishop of Verona in 360. He was also to become patron saint of Verona. Not only did he write fervent homilies, he was also a fierce enemy of paganism and, as such, has the honour ascribed to him of having converted the peoples of the Venetian area to Christianity. His feast day is celebrated 12 April.

Above, episodes from the portal of San Zeno: left St. Zeno, whilst fishing in the Adige River, receives the messengers of king Gallienus asking him to exorcise the king's daughter who was possessed by a demon; center, the prophet Balaam riding a donkey; right, the Sacrifice of Isaac.

Inside view of the basilica.

Complete view of the magnificent portal with the bronze plates. The extreme detail characterising this precious work of art can be admired on the opposite page in the ornamentation surrounding the figure of Nebuchadnezzar. This goes back to the 12th century.

may well be even older. It was later turned into an altar and put in the centre of the presbytery where it can still be admired today as one of the extremely rare examples of early sculpture in Verona. The centre of the crypt corresponds to the main apse. Here the *mortal remains of Saint Zeno* are revered, kept as they are in a large glass reliquary. They were found again in 1838 and wrapped in bishop's dress with the face being covered by a silver mask. The left aisle of the church preserves another important piece of sculpture, the large porphyritic cup which is believed to have belonged to the Roman thermal baths together with the one which is now an integral part of the fountain in Piazza delle Erbe. The basilica is also important for its precious cycles of paintings decorating its walls and going back to the thirteenth and fourteenth centuries. The artists who created them remained perhaps unknown, but they were indeed capable of illustrating the evolution of art in Verona from the earliest of times, characterised by moving expressive naivety, right through to the all too evident influence of Giotto and the school of Altichiero. Critics generally refer to these unnamed artists as the First, Second and Third Master of Saint Zeno. Some fresco paintings are particularly noteworthy, such as the gigantic fourteenth-century *Saint Cristopher, Our Lady*

The triptych with *Our Lady sitting on throne between angels and saints*, masterpiece by Andrea Mantegna.

The spacious, austere Romanesque cloister of San Zeno going back to the 12th century. Closed in by a long uninterrupted series of small double columns, the cloister holds some ancient treasures, such as that of Giuseppe della Scala, not to mention some interesting frescoes. The view of the cloister looking towards the side of San Zeno with the bell tower dominating is particularly beautiful.

in white, the *Crucifixion, Saint Steven, Saint George* and *Christ's Baptism*. It is, however, the overall pictorial atmosphere evoked by the group of frescoes together which impress the visitor, especially in the scratched on signatures and the chronicle-like annotations on the history of Verona going back to the remotest of times. The huge fresco painted in the upper section of the presbytery and dated 1397 depicts *Our Lady sitting on a throne and Saints*. It is a work by Altichiero's studio. Dating back to the middle of the same century there is a large *Stational Cross* painted on wood. By far the most important work housed in Saint Zeno is without doubt the famous triptych by Andrea Mantegna. This priceless piece represents *Our Lady sitting on a throne between angels and saints*. It was created in 1459 and constitutes one of the cornerstones of Renaissance painting in the Veneto region. Its predellae represent the *Prayer in the garden*, the *Crucifixion* and the *Resurrection*. They are, however, only copies made in the nineteenth century to substitute the originals which had been taken to France under Napoleon and never returned. Today they are at the Louvre and the Museum of Tours. Lying right next to the basilica there is the spacious Romanesque **cloister** dating back to the twelfth century. The portico is measured out in a long series of small double columns supporting small arches which alternate between being round and ogival from side to side. The northern side opens out into an elegant, square based appendix, a small *shrine* which once covered one of the wells of the abbey. The entire portico houses very old tombs such as the one opened in 1313 for the Della Scala family. It also holds noteworthy thirteenth-century frescoes.

San Bernardino

The **church and monastery of Saint Bernardino** were built in the middle of the fifteenth century by Giovanni da Capistrano. Though terribly damaged during the last world war, today they have been perfectly restored. They do not, however, have their original choir and presbytery, not to mention the frescoes which once embellished them by Michele da Verona. These have unfortunately been lost forever. The façade in brickwork is preceded by a noteworthy *cloister* and is decorated with Gothic pinnacles high on the top and at the extremities. The *portal* dates back to 1474 and is surmounted by *statues of Saint Bonaventure, Saint Bernardino and Saint Anthony. Saint Francis receiving the stigmata* is represented in the lunette. The inside consists in a nave twice the size of its single side aisle. The aisle, in fact, is an addition built slightly later in 1486 so as to allow for the opening of the chapels. The chapels in turn also offer up certain surprising treasures. The first chapel on the right holds frescoes by Nicolò Giolfino depicting *Stories of Saint John, Christ among prophets and Apostles* and *Stories of Saint Francis.* The *Pellegrini Chapel* is a real delight inasmuch as it is preceded by an atrium with a barrel-vault which was designed by Sanmicheli in 1529 and executed on a circular plan. The plan itself envisaged an intriguing correspondence coming into play among the variously sized niches. The fluted Corinthian columns in turn confer the entire setting of the chapel with fascinating elegance. And in amongst the paintings by Morone, Caroto and Benaglio, by far the most salient and beautiful element is the *"Morone Room"* which can be reached through the convent. This room was originally a library brought about by the Sagramoso Family in 1493. The room owes its name to the large fresco cycles decorating it. These frescoes were painted between 1494 and 1503 by Domenico Morone, his son Francesco and helpers from his studio. The walls hold frescoes marvellously depicting *Saints of the Franciscan Order, Franciscan Martyrs of Morocco, Saints Anthony from Padua, Bonaventure, Bernardino and Ludovico from Toulouse.* On the bottom wall there is the fresco *Saint Francis and Saint Clare presenting Lionello Sagramoso and his wife Anna Tramarino to Our Lady.* Sagramoso and his wife had commissioned the fresco cycles.

Views of the fifteenth century Chiesa di San Bernardino, painstakingly restored after the destruction of the last war: the simple façade, the splendid dome with caisson ceiling and one of the niches refining the circular Pellegrini Chapel by Sanmicheli and the large cloister of the ancient monastery.

Around the walls of Verona

The **walls of Verona** offer without a doubt an interesting walk around the city. The first wall was erected to protect Verona in Roman times and only had two gates. Many centuries later, the Della Scala family built a wider ring around the city so as to contain the entire urban context. This included its many fortresses, amongst which *Castel San Pietro* which was demolished in the nineteenth century due to its threatening strategic position. These walls were then substantially strengthened but left practically unaltered when the city was under Venetian rule. It was under the French and the Austrians centuries later that major alteration was carried out on the walls. Between the twelfth and thirteenth centuries, therefore, on the other side of the Adige river around the hill of St. Peter's, development was well underway in what was to become the Castle Quarter. New fortifications, called **Muri Novi**, were built around this nucleus. The new fortifications were not built, however, in the typical Roman style with square walls. The new ones followed and accentuated the natural characteristics of the terrain. The

Views of a segment of the walls which still stretch out around Verona:
above, the walls near the Gran Guardia; below, Porta Vescovo.

method involved was called *a sacco*, that is, "filling" whereby two external walls were built not more than a metre apart with the area in between becoming then filled in with river stones, broken bricks and roof tiles together with already used stone building material. All this was cemented together with soft-setting mortar. The external containing walls were, instead, built in medium sized stone blocks which, though not perfectly hewn into squares, were firmly cemented together with hard-setting mortar. The towers built for defence were not evenly spaced out from each other. What dictated their positioning was a matter of contingent strategy.

Above, Porta Palio; below, Porta Nuova.

There also existed some isolated or advance defence posts around the inhabited areas such as those of Saint Zeno and Saint Steven. In such cases, the defence measures were palisades or fences made of wood, preceded by a ditch or moat and reinforced with small brick towers. The entire city wall cannot be considered later than thirteenth-century. The gates, on the other hand, date back to the sixteenth century except for the older Porta dei Leoni and Porta Borsari. **Porta San Giorgio** is to the north of the city next to the rampart by the same name. The walls then wind their way past another fortress, *Castel San Felice*, which was begun by the Visconti family but completed by the Venetians. Then comes **Porta San Zeno** which has three barrel-vaults and is made in stone and brick. **Porta Vescovo** is analogous in structure and was restored by the Austrian government. Other interesting parts of the city wall follow, such as the more recent **Porta della Vittoria Nuova** which was planned and built by Giuseppe Barbieri in 1837. The erection of this new gate made it necessary to close the older Della Scala gate. The walk around the walls and the series of ramparts of Verona ends with three other gates: **Porta Nuova**, planned by Sanmicheli but widened in the nineteenth century via the addition of the two lateral barrel-vaults; **Porta Palio**, formerly Porta San Sisto, which owes its name to the traditional *palio* or horse competition which was run in the city; **Porta Fura** or **Catena** which has the characteristic of being articulated into three barrel-vaults each of a different period. Porta Palio deserves a special mention, primarily because it is considered to be Sanmicheli's absolute masterpiece in the field of military architecture. It was created around the middle of the sixteenth century with a characteristic: the side looking outside the city and the side looking in towards the city have two completely different physiognomies. The side looking outwards has only one opening but is subdivided by couples of columns and covered with smooth, austere ashlar-work. The side looking inwards is more elegant in its respect of tendentially classical canons. It is comprised of five barrel-vaults which provide light for the tunnel behind them.

La Porta dei Leoni

La **Porta dei Leoni** or Leona (Lion or "Leona" Gate) gets its name from the sculptures decorating the tympanum of a Roman tomb discovered nearby. Unlike the Borsari Gate, this gate no longer has one of its barrel-vaults. The one still surviving does not open towards the country but, rather, towards the nearby *Forum* or square which can just be seen at the end of the great *Cardo*. Both careful excavations and an intelligent display of the base of one of the towers have been carried out. A circular wall made of one and a half feet long bricks, together with the remains of the flooring and hydraulic system, runs two metres underneath the current street level which has risen over the centuries due to the deposits left by the Adige river often in flood. What remains of the Lion Gate (practically only half of the original monument) gives us an idea of its original elegance and size. It is, perhaps, by the same architect who erected the Borsari Gate. In this case, however, it is extremely likely that he transformed a pre-existing building. To distinguish them, the third level became instrumental inasmuch as it did not appear to be the repetition of the second line of windows but presented, instead, a four-sided figure within the central concave part. It is thought to have been planned to create architectural movement within an otherwise empty space or, perhaps, to have housed sculpture. Another characteristic of the Lion Gate is its second *wall* in brick which has been used as a wall for centuries for the house built onto it whose marble door seems to be leaning on it. The wall is, however, one of the last vestiges of the older city gate. It goes back to the Republican age (first century BC) and is simpler and more austere.

CHURCH OF SAINTS FERMO AND RUSTICO
(San Fermo Maggiore)

The particular Gothic style peculiar to Verona predominates by far in the **Church of Saints Fermo and Rustico** on the banks of the Adige river. This Gothic style derives from the Romanesque of the evocative underground church which had been built over a sacred building going back to the eighth century. This earlier church in turn had probably substituted a small fifth-century Christian temple which popular devotion had raised in memory of the place where the two saints had supposedly undergone their martyrdom in 361. The *lower church* of Benedictine foundation goes back to the eleventh century and supports the upper Basilica in which the Romanesque elements can be detected in the secondary apses, the presbytery, in the base of the bell-tower and in the façade. These elements must have been completed by the thirteenth century. With the advent of the Franciscans in 1313, the single-nave church was enlarged and transformed into a Gothic temple. Pinnacles, brick-work, stone cornices, an unusual criss-crossing of yellow and pink

Although only the left-hand side of the inner part remains, the Porta dei Leoni still gives us an idea today of the might of this veritable bastion which had two barrel-vaults.

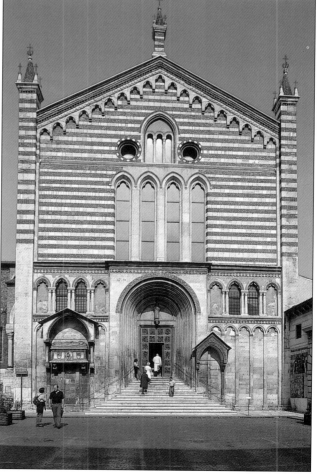

The magnificent Chiesa dei Santi Fermo e Rustico, or better known as San Fermo Maggiore. The tomb of Giovanni da Tolentino with protyron and the monument to Aventino Fracastoro stand out on the façade.

stripes, crosses and palmettes in wrought iron, the large side *portal* in polychromatic marble and an extremely high protyron, not to mention a wooden hull-like ceiling, all add up to create a building of rare beauty. The *façade* is substantially Romanesque in design with a loggia and four large one-light windows which anticipate its hut-like termination. On the right the façade supports the hanging protyron of the *tomb of Giovanni da Tolentino*, whereas on the left it supports the ostentatious **funeral monument to Aventino Fracastoro**, doctor to the Della Scala family who died in 1368. Behind its doors, the basilica holds many paintings and sculptures going back to various moments in history. These include the group *Mourning over the dead Christ* by Giovanni Rigino and the *funeral monument to Nicolò Brenzoni*, a work by the Florentine Nanni di Bartolo. Around the urn a group of statues depict the *Resurrection*, while on the wall behind it, on the inside of the cornice surrounding the sculptures, Pisanello painted the *Annunciation* – not only one of the finest works by this particular

Even though the main apse is also truly Gothic, the apsidioles are, however, substantially Romanesque.

The area around the apse with the large architectural structure surrounding the choir, and the *Crucifixion* attributed to Turone, but by some attributed instead to Altichiero.

artist but a masterpiece of the entire international Gothic movement in painting. Though varying both in style and historical period, every single intervention seems to fit perfectly into this setting. A case in point is the *decoration around the choir* which closes off the main altar. Though embellished with the frescoes above of a Giottesque matrix and depicting *Prior Daniele Gusmerio* and *Guglielmo di Castelbarco*, the fourteenth-century choir blends in perfectly well with the Renaissance *monument to the Della Torre family*, a work by Andrea Briosco, called il Riccio. The large 1360 *pulpit* is also noteworthy with its Gothic canopy and surround-

The evocative lower church closed by cross vaults supported by square and cross-shaped pilasters. It still holds numerous interesting frescoes datable between the 11th and 13th centuries. To the left the Baptism of Christ is exceptionally interesting in its austere simplicity.

Preceding page: tomb of Niccolò Brenzoni, made in the first half of the fifteenth century by Nanni di Bartolo and framed above by the *Annunciation* by Pisanello.

ing frescoes by Martino da Verona. In the right transept an *Our Lady and Saints* by Battista Dal Moro can be seen together with a *Crucifixion* by Brusasorci. In the left transept, instead, Giottesque-style frescoes telling *Stories about Saint Francis* can be admired together with *Saints Anthony, Nicholas and Augustine* by Liberale da Verona. On the right wall, at the altar of the chapel of Our Lady, il Caroto placed his *Mary, Saint Anna and Saints Sebastian, Rocco, Peter and John the Baptist*. The inner side of the façade holds a lunette containing a 1363 fresco attributed to Turone depicting the *Crucifixion*. The lower church is in the form of the Latin cross with a central nave, two aisles and cross vaults. The walls and pillars, which are characterised by archaic capitals, display numerous frescoes datable between the eleventh and thirteenth centuries.

The Civic Museum of Natural History

Michele Sanmicheli created one of his architectural masterpieces on the Lungadige Porta Vittoria, **Palazzo Lavezola Pompei**. He probably built it around the middle of the sixteenth century. Its peculiar characteristic is the obvious asymmetry of the courtyard with respect to the central axis of the building itself. The *ground floor* has the usual ashlar-work covering and cambered windows of the period. The *"piano nobile"*, instead, is greatly embellished by the elegant loggia onto which seven windows open separated by Doric half-columns which support the cornice above. This residence was destined to house the **Civic Museum of Natural History**. This is one of the richest museums of this kind not only in Italy, but in all of Europe. Here there are geological models and research laboratories, together with nineteen rooms displaying large collections of varying sorts. These include fossil fauna and flora from Mount Bolca, mineral, zoological and botanical collections, collections of palaeontological interest and others still regarding the Veneto area in pre-historical times including Bronze-Age findings from the area of Lake Garda. The fossil collection is truly incredible in both quantity and variety. In the section dedicated to fauna and spread out in several different rooms, the fascinating collection boasts exemplars of both local and exotic mammals and birds, amphibians and reptiles. Interesting is the typical population of the Quaternary period as it might have been in the Veneto area including the cave bear, the elk and the elegant huge deer.

The Giusti Garden

Palazzo Giusti del Giardino is a magnificent town dwelling built at the end of the sixteenth century in the typical horse-shoe shape which characterised such suburban villas. It has elegant architectural structures built in and fine artistic points to its merit such as the noteworthy *façade* painted by Orazio Farinati in 1591 and the internal *frescoes* by Francesco Lorenzi and Lodovico Dorigny. Its main claim to glory is, however, its magnificent *gardens* which were probably planned and set out around 1580 in line with the main entrance. The gardens had a quadrangular layout with perpendicular pathways crossing at the centre. They thus constitute a fine example indeed of an Italian-style garden to which Luigi Trezza added, in 1786, a suggestive labyrinth in box-wood. A delightful avenue of cypress trees leads to the cliff which closes off the gardens to the north. Five grottos can still be seen in the cliff, the largest of which opens out under a belvedere terrace and was once decorated with shells, mother-of-pearl, coral and coloured glass. The mirrors were also originally placed here to create an optical illusion – it would seem to the visitor to be looking out over a much wider visual field. Today it is possible to visit the gardens and enjoy what is considered to be one of the greenest and most fascinating corners of Verona.

The Museo Civico di Storia Naturale, housed in the Palazzo Lavezola Pompei built by Sanmicheli.

The splendid, luxuriant Giusti Gardens.

Santa Maria in Organo

An old Benedictine abbey dating back very probably to the eighth century once looked out directly onto the river. This was **Santa Maria in Organo** which was originally built outside the city walls. It was re-built in the twelfth century but was to take on the physiognomy we know it for today only towards the end of the fifteenth century. This was thanks to the Olivetan Fathers living there in that period. It was Michele Sanmicheli who covered the original Romanesque-Gothic *façade* with the new lower part. He created this lower part in white marble articulating it into three arcades divided by half-columns and pilaster strips. The portal dates to 1592. The upper part of the façade still shows its fourteenth-century structure in tufa and brickwork with the typical decoration in small hanging arches. The *bell-tower*, instead, in due to the craftsmanship of Francesco da Castello, but was designed by fra Giovanni da Verona and completed in 1533. The *inside* of the church presents the form of a Latin cross with the presbytery raised above the crypt. It also contains noteworthy works of art, especially frescoes. The walls of the nave were completely fresco-painted in the sixteenth century with *Stories from Genesis and the Old Testament* (Nicolò Giolfino worked on the right wall while Giovan Francesco Caroto, helped by Giovanni Caroto, worked on the right wall). They both worked on the apse and the presbytery. Domenico Morone and his helpers worked on the dome and the transept in 1498. The detached frescoes depicting *Saints Peter Martyr and Francis* are by Francesco Torbido, whereas the *Santa Francesca Romana* is by Guercino (1639). The elegant wooden *choir* was splendidly carved at the end of the fifteenth century by the able hands of fra Giovanni da Verona. Twenty years later the same artist was to create the wooden back piece in the sacristy. A visit down to the *crypt* is certainly evocative. It is a fascinating, yet austere example of pre-Romanesque architecture, where capitals dating back to the eighth century and, therefore, to the original construction, can still be admired.

The characteristic façade of Santa Maria in Organo.

Shots of the vaults and frescoes richly decorating the central nave, the apse, the transept and the dome of Santa Maria in Organo.

The Church of Saints Nazaro and Celso

The **Church of Saints Nazaro and Celso** was built between 1464 and 1483 on the site of a holy building from the eighth century and as part of an ancient Benedictine monastery. Today the entrance to it is through an elegant *courtyard* decorated in exhedrae preceded by a monumental portal built in 1688. The church has an austere but agile *façade* in brick with large Renaissance windows. The *bell-tower* was built in 1552. Inside the church there is a nave and two aisles laterally surrounded by an interesting series of chapels and ending in three apses. Of particular interest there is the *Cappella Maggiore* enriched by the *frescoes* by Farinati and the polyptych divisions by Bartolomeo Montagna depicting *saint Benedict, the Baptist and saints Nazaro and Celso*. In the *Cappella di San Biagio* (chapel to St. Blaise) in the left wing of the church the highly individual architectural taste displayed reflects the personality of its creator, the Lombard artist Beltramo di Valsolda. Though finished in 1488, the chapel was only consecrated in 1529. The marvellously frescoed walls depict the *Storie di San Biagio* (stories of St. Blaise) by the painter Bartolomeo Montagna (1504-1505). The dome was decorated instead by Giovanni Maria Falconetto and Domenico Morone. On the superb marble *altar* there is the *Arca dei Santi Biagio e Giuliana* (tomb of saints Blaise and Giuliana) by Bernardino Panteo (1508). The altar piece with the *Martirio dei Santi Biagio e Giuliana* (martyrdom of saints Blaise and Giuliana) by Bonsignori and the **predella** by Girolamo dai Libri are also magnificent.

In the *sacristy* fine fifteenth century cupboards of inlaid wood can be admired. There is also a triptych with the *Pietà* and *St. Benedict and St. Francis* (fifteenth century). *Our Lady and Saints* is by Brusasorci, not to mention the polytych divisions by Bartolomeo Montagna depicting *Santi Biagio e Giuliana* (Saints Blaise and Giuliana) and *Cristo sul Sepolcro* (Christ on the sepulchre).

The seventeenth century portal leading to the great courtyard in front of the Chiesa dei Santi Nazaro e Celso and the bright façade in brick, on which two large Renaissance windows open.

The Church of San Giovanni in Valle

This charming **church dedicated to St. John** is the result of the re-building in tufa of the eighth century church destroyed by an earthquake in 1117. The original church had been built on an ancient Christian cemetery. The church thus took on the characteristic elements of Veronese Romanesque. Though seriously damaged during the Second World War, the church still proudly stands with its nave and two aisles each ending in an apse. Its simple *façade* is decorated with a central mullioned window and a hanging *protyron*

The Chiesa di San Giovanni in Valle, with its simple façade embellished by the presence of the protyron which closes off the lunette where Stefano da Verona painted an Our Lady and Saints.

Below, the modern elegant buildings of the Verona Fair (Fiera di Verona).

which begins the portal. In the lunette it was most probably Stefano da Verona who painted in the first half of the fifteenth century the artistic image of *Madonna e Santi* which can still be admired today. A peculiar characteristic of this church is the main nave which is narrower than the two aisles from which it is separated by a series of pillars and columns. Two Roman-Christian fourth century *sarcophagi* in the crypt prove that classical culture actually lived on and renewed itself continually within the new and ever-stronger cultural environment afforded by Christianity. One of the sarcophagi bears figures in high-relief enacting *episodes from the Gospels.* Its lid instead is Gothic, added in 1395. It bears images of *St. Simon* and *St. Judas* which gave the sarcophagus its name. The second sarcophagus shows the portraits of a deceased couple closed within a shell placed above a pastoral scene and the portraits of *St. Peter* and *St. Paul.* It is possible to enter the *crypt* via the raised presbytery whose magnificent frescoes were completely damaged in the last war. The crypt is important because of the eighth century walls contained within, together with columns from the ninth century, which are the last remaining vestiges of the early Christian church.
On the outside, there are the remains of a Romanesque *cloister* and a tall, four-sided Romanesque *bell tower.* The spire and bell chamber were added in the eighteenth century. The *apses* of the church are particularly noteworthy inasmuch as the largest one is crowned in arches with a sculptured frieze of hunting scenes within spiralling motifs.

The Fair

One of the most functional and well-known buildings in Verona is without a doubt the so-called **Fiera** or "Fair". Not far from Porta Nuova, this is practically an entire city quarter which represents a huge, well-equipped infrastructure built at the end of the nineteenth century as a pavilion for the six-monthly horse market. In 1930, however, it was handed over to a specific autonomous body responsible for the organisation of exhibitions, conventions and fairs. Today it houses in its pavilions an interesting *Old Carriage Museum* with nineteenth-century Italian carriages. The organisation governing the Fair periodically organises world events from "Vinitaly" to the extremely popular "International Fair of Agriculture and Zootechnics". It still regularly offers an entire series of exhibitions specific to this sector, including machinery and agricultural products, and beyond, such as the specialised activities in agricultural food produce. It varies throughout the year and deals with a wide range of products in the fields of herbal and thermal activity. Now it also deals with the fascinating world of marble.

The Sanctuary of Our Lady of Lourdes

The hill of San Leonardo is a strategically important plateau dominating the city. In 1838 it was chosen by the Archduke Maximilian Habsburg as the perfect site for an austere military fortress. For more than a century the fortress was used as a jail for political prisoners. In 1958, the hundredth anniversary of the first apparition of Our Lady in Lourdes, it was decided that the old military building should given over to the Padri Stimmatini (Fathers of the Stigmata). These monks had practically been left without a house after the bombing of the Second World War had destroyed the Church of Saint Theresa. It was in 1958 that the architect Paolo Rossi was entrusted with the task of transforming the fortress into a sanctuary. After six years of work the **Sanctuary of Our Lady of Lourdes** was born. Reinforced concrete was intelligently used to create its elegant structure which is characterised by a superb circular body and two protruding wings. In a modern grotto reminiscent of the much older one in the Church of Saint Theresa, the Padri Stimmatini placed the venerated *statue of Our Lady* created by Ugo Zannoni in 1908 and miraculously rescued intact from the ruins after the war. The sanctuary seems to be looking over the city of Verona. In fact, judging from the number of pilgrims winding their way up to this sanctuary, it can easily be gleaned that the sanctuary is now the object of popular devotion.

The Sanctuary of Our Lady of Lourdes dominates Verona and the Adige River from the hill of Colle di San Leonardo.
It represents a revered place of worship and is the object of much popular devotion.

AROUND VERONA

Not far from Verona, wedged into the corner formed by the regions of Lombardy, Veneto, and Trentino-Alto Adige, is the most extensive lacustrine basin in all Italy and one of the largest sub-Alpine lakes: Lake Garda, with its 370 square kilometers and its lightsome shore towns, is a far-famed tourist playground— besides one of the most charming sites along the entire arc of the Alps. It wasn't by chance, then, that Virgil sang the beauty of its turquoise waters perennially rippled by the breezes and of the changing but always suggestive scenery that creates its now subdued, now dramatic setting. That the shores of the lake were colonized in ancient times by the Veneti, the Ligurians, the Etruscans, and the Gauls only attests to how its mild climate, its fertile land, and its waters abounding in fish have always attracted people and offered excellent conditions for populous settlements.
The major towns on the Lombard side of the lake are **Desenzano**, **Salò**, **Gardone**, and **Limone**—and of course **Sirmione**, the "gem of peninsulas" according to Virgil and a favorite vacation spot even in Roman times. The town is set at the tip of a slender point reaching out into the center of the lake; at its tip is a high vantage point dominated by the majestic fortifications and the fascinating medieval *Rocca Scaligera*. **Peschiera**, farther to the east, also of Roman origin but fortified by the Venetians, has always been a busy fishing and trading port, lying in a cradle of hills that slope gently downward toward the plain of the Po river valley. On the Venetian shore are the lovely and very ancient **Bardolino**, a well-known health resort cradled by luxuriant vineyards that produce the famous wine of the same name, the elegant **Garda**, with its picturesque bay and the many parks in its flourishing cen-

Malcesine as seen from the cable cars which run along Monte Baldo.

ter, which has been settled since the prehistoric era, and **Torri del Benaco**, a vacation spot of considerable importance at the foot of the majestic mountain chain that culminates in **Monte Baldo**. This is one of the most notable mountain formations in the entire Garda territory, and a sort of unequaled natural terrace offering unique and wide-ranging views. This is the place for unforgettable walks in an uncontaminated natural environment, where we can admire the surprising abundance of the local flora, famous for its great variety and its many rare species of plants. In wintertime, when its slopes are mantled in snow, Monte Baldo also offers well-equipped ski facilities that attract hordes of winter sports fans. At the foot of the mountain, facing north, set in a bezel of the green of the woods and the blue of the lake, is **Malcesine**, under

Garda: panorama of the town looking out onto the gulf.

Peschiera: a view towards the port.

the *Castello Scaligero*. The luminous beauty of this lovely locality enticed, enchanted, and finally won over one of the 18th's century's most famous tourists: Wolfgang Goethe, who, in mid-September 1786 during his celebrated *Italian Journey*, traveled through the area.

INDEX